The Art of Glass

Integrating Architecture and Glass

Stephen Knapp

ROCKPORT
PUBLISHERS

Rockport Publishers
Gloucester, Massachusetts

First published in the United States of America by
Rockport Publishers, Inc.
33 Commercial Street
Gloucester, Massachusetts 01930-5089
Telephone: (978) 282-9590
Fax: (978) 283-2742

Distributed to the book trade and art trade in the United States by
North Light Books, an imprint of
F & W Publications
1507 Dana Avenue
Cincinnati, Ohio 45207
Telephone: (800) 289-0963

Cover photo: Refractive glass wall, First Hawaiian Bank;
James Carpenter, glass artist; David Franzen, photographer.

Other Distribution by
Rockport Publishers
Gloucester, Massachusetts 01930-5089

ISBN 1-56496-343-8

10 9 8 7 6 5 4 3 2 1

Designer: Beth Santos Design

Printed in Hong Kong by Midas Printing Limited.

Acknowledgments

This book is a tribute to all those involved in The Art of Glass—all who create, fabricate, install, support, or encourage architectural art glass. I want to thank those at Rockport Publishers who have helped put together this book: Stan Patey, Winnie Danenbarger, and Rosalie Grattaroti, for believing in this project; and Todd Crane and Martha Wetherill, for their contributions to the process. Edward R. Burian should be thanked for his contributions to Joanne Stuhr's essay.

Those artists and friends who have ensured that this book was complete and who supported my involvement in glass include Ed Carpenter, Lutz Haufschild, Beth Hylen, John and Goldi Luebtow, Gabriel Mayer of Franz Mayer, Munich, Germany, Andrew Moor, Takako Sano, Dick Schulze, Rick and Cathy Shaw, Johannes Schreiter, Ana Thiel, Gerard Walsh, David Wilson, Dave Banks, Ted Polenski, Wilhelm and Barbara Derix, and Irene M. Molitor at Derix Studios, Jean Jacques Duval, Dick Millard, the Glass Art Society. I'd especially like to thank my children, Sarah and Jonathan, who have been more than understanding of their dad's life as an artist, and my wife, Frankie, who organized the submissions for this book and encouraged other artists. In her job "in charge of everything else," she manages my studio, and makes my life whole. Thanks to you all.

About the Author

Stephen Knapp, internationally renowned for his large-scale works of art in public, corporate, and private collections, works in kiln-formed, dichroic, and cast glass, and in metal, stone, mosaic, and ceramic. He frequently writes and lectures on architecture. His work has appeared in numerous international publications, including *Art & Antiques*, *Architectural Record*, *Honoho Geijutsu*, *Identity*, *Interior Design*, *Interiors*, *Nikkei Architecture*, *Progressive Architecture*, and the *New York Times*.

Contents

Introduction by Stephen Knapp   6

Glass and Architecture   10
Essay by Joanne Stuhr

Berin Behn and Jan Aspinall   14
Australia

Alexander Beleschenko   18
United Kingdom

Joel Berman   22
Canada

Leifur Breidfjord   26
Iceland

Wilhelm Buschulte   30
Germany

Ed Carpenter   34
United States

James Carpenter   38
United States

Warren Carther   42
Canada

José Fernández Castrillo   46
Spain

Brian Clarke   50
United Kingdom

Martin Donlin   54
United Kingdom

Bert Glauner   58
Mexico

Karl-Martin Hartmann   62
Germany

Lutz Haufschild   66
Canada

Gordon Huether   70
United States

Graham Jones   74
United Kingdom

Shelley Jurs   78
United States

Keshava (Antonio Sainz)   82
Spain

Joachim Klos   86
Germany

Stephen Knapp   90
United States

John Gilbert Luebtow   94
United States

Maureen McGuire   98
United States

Paul Marioni and Ann Troutner   102
United States

Jean Myers   106
United States

David Pearl   110
United Kingdom

Jochem Poensgen   114
Germany

Narcissus Quagliata   118
Italy

Maya Radoczy   122
United States

José Antonio Rage Mafud   126
Mexico

Ludwig Schaffrath   130
Germany

Johannes Schreiter   134
Germany

Jeff G. Smith   138
United States

Arthur Stern   142
United States

Raquel Stolarski-Assael   146
Mexico

Karl-Heinz Traut   150
Germany

Kenneth vonRoenn   154
United States

David Wilson   158
United States

Gallery of Artists   162

Directory of Artists   174

Photo Credits   176

Introduction

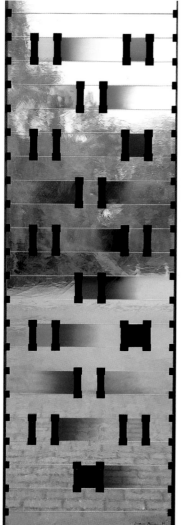

Alchemy, mystery, magic, and transformation—the luminous poetry of glass presents both a spiritual and physical presence. From its early discovery, shrouded in apocryphal myths in the ancient landscape of the Middle East, to its contemporary status as multidimensional commodity, it has inspired and provoked. Today's architectural glass, with whole facades of seemingly static flatness, is in stark contrast to the glass used as art in the cathedrals and churches of the Middle Ages. Although critiqued and maligned for its banality, contemporary glass changes all day long, displaying light, movement, and color. The reflected dialogue that buildings have with one another, pleasantly distorted by minute deflections in large sheets of glass, has added a touch of whimsy to our built environment. Architectural art glass, which ventures far beyond everyday architectural glazing, filters, moves, and transforms light, altering the spaces it seeks to contain. Changed by the light it manipulates, its lyrical and contemplative qualities make it an ideal foil for the bustle of today.

Architectural art glass experienced a brief revival at the turn of the century with the work of Louis Comfort Tiffany in the United States, and that of the Dutchman Thorn Prikker in Germany. Tiffany's work, painterly and almost separated from the architecture, required the development of new techniques for the surface treatment of glass. Prikker's style, geometric, abstract, and driven by the architecture, worked with the hard edge of the glass and the lead-line. It took stained glass away from the traditional church window designs and moved the collaborative process to a position of prominence.

Architects Frank Lloyd Wright in the United States, Charles Rennie Mackintosh in Scotland, and Antoni Gaudí in Spain designed stained glass for their buildings. Matisse, Chagall, and Braque also completed architectural commissions in stained glass. In the Bauhaus, Paul Klee and Josef Albers worked in stained glass, pushing the vernacular still further.

It was not until after World War II, however, when postwar Germany had more churches and public buildings to rebuild than ever before, that architectural art glass came into its own. The country, intent on looking forward, was receptive to new ideas, and thus became fertile ground for a new generation of glass artists. Georg Meistermann was the first of these artists, building on the pioneering advances of Thorn Prikker while becoming more spontaneous. He was followed by Ludwig Schaffrath, Johannes Schreiter, Wilhelm Buschulte, Jochem Poensgen, Hans Gottfried von

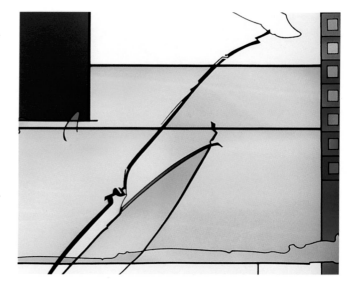

Stockhausen, and others. This German movement of postwar art glass has been the most influential, with Schaffrath and Schreiter at the forefront, as they explored designs that went beyond the rectangle to become an organic presence. Schaffrath's early work shows Meistermann's influence, but he soon developed his own style. His strong sense of movement, with parallel lines carrying amorphous shapes through geometric spaces, moved art glass to the next plane. Dynamic and forceful, his work brought drama to architecture. Johannes Schreiter is noted for his unorthodox use of the lead-line, letting it play across the surface, counterpoint to a strong sense of space. His striking compositions often use opaque glass designed to be transfused by light. Both he and Schaffrath have been fascinated with the manipulation of light and the effect it has on the viewer.

In the United States after World War II, the work of Robert Sowers, particularly the monumental installation at the American Airlines terminal at Kennedy International Airport in New York, was extremely influential. His books, *The Lost Art* and *Stained Glass: An Architectural Art*, were available when a resurgence of contemporary crafts in the late 1960s and early 1970s converged with a demanding Post-Modern architectural movement whose proponents sought to embellish buildings and were, if not eager to collaborate with artists, at least willing to explore the possibilities.

Following Sowers, the most influential glass artists of the contemporary era in the United States have been the unrelated Carpenters, Ed Carpenter and James Carpenter, working in syncopated acts of discovery on opposite coasts. Ed shows how an integrated piece of art can work on a large scale, becoming a dynamic signature with the architecture. James's dichroic installations demonstrate how light can enter a space to be a potent force. In postwar England, the painter John Piper collaborated with glass artist Patrick Reyntiens. Brian Clarke, strongly influenced by both Piper and Schreiter, is one of the most prolific artists working in architectural glass today. His experience as a painter helps in the formation of his glass, as it is shaped by his dialogue with architects and their buildings.

One of the most influential forces in modern art glass has been the German atelier approach, which allows artists to reach beyond what they or their assistants could do with their own hands. Not limited by their own ability or knowledge, they could call upon a broad base of talented craftsmen in various studios to execute their visions. Widely used in Europe, this was soon emulated by other artists who came to Germany to study under the masters, and it has had a major effect on the size and scale of architectural art glass.

This freedom to design and create, unrestricted by the limits of the craft, has led to an unprecedented use of new techniques and technology in art glass. Plate glass became a carrier for laminated jewels, bevels, and cast and colored glasses. Mechanically produced glasses were added to the traditional stained glasses, and sandwiches of float glass and stained glass, marbles, and crushed glass entered the vernacular. Carved, multiple layers of laminated glass, acid-polished glass, silk-screened glass, and dichroics appeared.

There are yet other artists whose approach to art glass makes them even more distinctive. Cast glass, which involves the shaping of hot glass into block form, produces an entirely different look, as evident in the work of the Czech couple Libensky and Brechtová. Their glass sculptures have long been revered in the West, but only recently have some of their magnificent architectural installations been photographed and displayed outside of their own country.

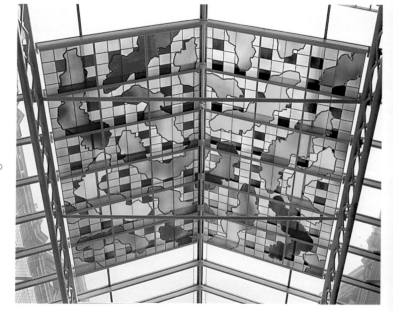

Kiln-formed glass, the process in which flat glass is heated over forms, is seen occasionally, but a small number of artists have developed it further, heating large sheets of plate glass to put bas-relief imagery into the glass. With its ability to show color in an ever-changing kinetic display of light and motion, kiln-formed glass may be the most perfect carrier for color. John Luebtow has taken it into a different dimension, with his massive sculptural pieces that are used as fountains and room dividers.

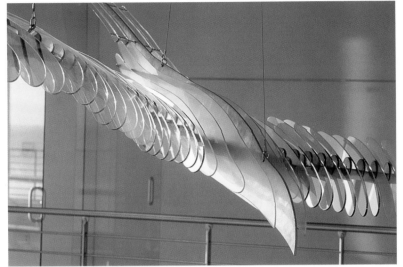

Today's glass artists demonstrate a startling range of technological innovations within each field. Many create sculpture, build furniture, develop lighting pieces, paint, and work with extensive types of materials. They consistently ignore the perceived separation of the fine and applied arts, and have developed tools that change the way they work on architectural projects.

Ironically, the growth of mechanized building systems, tight budgets, and a sharp increase in "value engineering" has fueled the demand for innovative architectural art glass. The need for meditative spaces and healing environments caused by information overload and the relentless pace of society has resulted in the use of art glass in the health care field, offices, public spaces, and homes. Shopping malls, which have replaced town squares as meeting places, look to art glass as another theatrical element that can attract customers.

Through all of this, the use of glass in the built environment has remained diverse, complex, and fluid. Just as it can function as a screen between two spaces, it can also be a bridge, bringing them together. Glass stops the eye and forces it beyond, often in the same piece. With symbolism and syllogism, it touches conscious thought and makes people pause. Elegant and ephemeral, its rhythms play across the human psyche and illuminate the soul.

Stephen Knapp

Glass and Architecture

"Architecture is the masterly, correct and magnificent play of masses brought together in light.
Our eyes are made to see forms in light, light and shade reveal these forms."
Le Corbusier, *Towards a New Architecture*, 1946

"Glass: air in air, to keep air out or keep it in."
Frank Lloyd Wright, *Wrightings and Buildings*, 1960

Architecture and glass have a long-standing partnership. Since its invention in pre-Roman times, glass has been used in buildings. And why not? It was a nearly miraculous substance that would let light in and keep the elements out. Even the earliest glass was clearer than alabaster, smoother and less fragile than mica, and it could be produced in larger sizes than either of its predecessors. Glass could be colored, colorless, opaque, translucent, or transparent; it could be painted, etched, ground, cut, leaded, stained, fused, bent, or carved like jewels (and that was just for windows). Large murals and mosaics were made of glass. Entire rooms were lined with glass fashioned to resemble agate or porphyry. Improved skills and technical advances allowed artisans to transform glass into furniture, floors, banisters, ceilings, and room dividers; virtually anything that could be imagined could be created from glass.

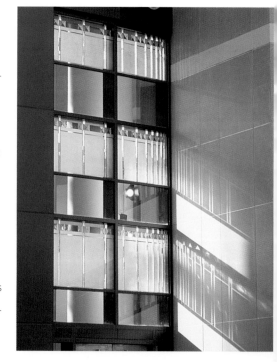

There have always been practical uses of glass within a building—penetration of light, illumination of surfaces, view of adjacent space, ventilation, and relief from claustrophobia. But there are philosophical, even psychological uses as well. As glass became a more familiar material, architects and artists began to incorporate it into buildings to achieve specific effects. Windows were used to track solar movements and astronomical events such as the alignment of planets (though in the Americas, this was practiced before glass was known). Generally, this was a reflection of the relationship between human ritual and celestial movement. Gothic architects used glass to depict spiritual symbolism. Careful placement provided

dramatic effects; soft light falling from high, clerestory windows or brilliant illumination of the altar in a dimly lit church could lift thoughts heavenward. To the Renaissance builder, tall, vertical windows suggested a physical manifestation of celestial, transcendent space—a miniature heaven on earth. Colored glass in window openings transformed light to create an ethereal atmosphere and to evoke a spiritual response. To achieve another type of illumination, stained glass scenes were commonly used in churches for didactic purposes when literacy rates were low.

Glass used as window provides a punched opening in the mass of a building, a piercing of the facade, a breaking out of the box. A window can be looked through or looked at, depending on placement and intent. It determines the focus and orientation of a room and its relationship to surrounding areas. It can function as lens, filter, or screen.

In the seventeenth and eighteenth centuries, position and form of windows reflected the intense drive to attain

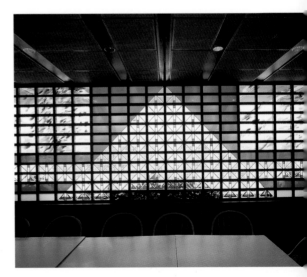

scientific information and to order and thereby control nature. Openings were conceived in such a way as to isolate nature, framing a carefully selected scene but keeping it at a safe distance. Separating the viewer from the view placed the human element in a position of superiority; one was a keen observer, not a participant. Small panes of glass were commonly used to create a grid across the vista as a reminder that indoor and outdoor were separate.

Nineteenth-century thinking about windows may best be summed up by a statement that Adolf Loos made to Le Corbusier: "A cultivated man does not look out of the window; his window is a ground glass; it is there only to let light in, not to let the gaze pass through." In the era of the birth of psychoanalysis, the gaze was a more introspective one, and architectural design, ever responsive to the changing demands and interests of contemporary society, used glass accordingly.

The contemporary view, by contrast, favors the integration of indoor and outdoor space. Windows are designed and placed in such a way that barriers disappear and the interior space is often saturated with light. People inside a building can see what takes place outside, just as easily as they themselves can be seen by people outside of the building. This change began in the nineteenth century and mirrored a radical shift in thinking about nature; no longer was one to remain a dispassionate observer. Because of Darwin and the Evolutionists, humans recognized themselves as a part of nature that is subject to, not master of, its laws, and buildings began to reflect that shift. The more modern architect sought to erase the division between inside and outside, to invite nature in.

Glass has always held a fascination for visionaries, artists and architects alike. Its qualities seem to inspire dreams. It is a solid liquid, its molten state imperceptible to the eye. It is hard, yet enormously fragile and therefore possesses an inherent danger. It embodies the phenomenon of transparency, both literally and figuratively. Such dreamers as Leonardo, Blake, and the Surrealists imagined towers made of glass. In the seventeenth century, glass enclosures were constructed to house exotic plants from foreign lands. The Crystal Palace, erected for the London World's Fair in 1851, was a dream which could, for the first time, be made real. 18,000 panes of glass were stretched across an elaborate system of trusses and girders.

Sixty years later, the poet Paul Scheerbart spoke for the German Expressionist architects about the importance of glass in social reform in his essay, "Glasarchitektur." He stated:

In order to raise our culture to a higher level, we are forced, whether we like it or not, to change our architecture. And this will be possible only if we free the rooms in which we live of their enclosed character. This, however, we can only do by introducing a glass architecture, which admits the light of the sun, of the moon, and of the stars into the rooms, not only through a few windows, but through as many walls as feasible, these to consist entirely of glass–colored glass.

More recently, Buckminster Fuller proposed to cover Manhattan with an enormous dome of glass. He dreamt: "From the inside there will be uninterrupted visual contact with the exterior world. The sun and moon will shine in the landscape and the sky will be completely visible, but the unpleasant effects of climate, heat, dust, bugs, glare, etc. will be modulated by the skin to provide a Garden of Eden interior."

The internal steel-truss frame was further developed in the twentieth century, which made possible two revolutionary changes that became the hallmarks of modern architecture: taller buildings (the skyscraper) and larger expanses of glass (the glass curtain). As Frank Lloyd Wright wrote, "No longer was the exterior wall the structural support that held up the building. An internal steel frame was the muscle." With this single technological improvement, architects could embrace the essence of modern thought—a nearly complete decomposition of surface. The building could almost disappear, leaving the pure form of only a framework to define space. The surrealist dream of the ideal building, one like ice, could become reality; Mies van der Rohe could construct his glass tower and Phillip Johnson could build his glass house. Now, dreams are limitless and anything can be made of glass.

Think of a building as a sculptural form, defined by its walls, existing in light and space. That form can be manipulated in certain ways. It can be pierced, punctured, or carved, allowing penetration into the interior or out to the exterior. It can be dissected or divided, which determines its movement and use. It can be connected to other forms, or isolated from them and adjacent space. Its mass can be lightened or increased by the materials from which it is made. It can be ornamented or decorated, inside or out, to soften or strengthen the form. Its function can be accentuated or hidden. Its dimensions, shape, surface, edge, color, texture, and pattern can be altered. As demonstrated in *The Art of Glass*, all of these effects can be accomplished with glass.

Joanne Stuhr
Curator of Exhibitions
Tucson Museum of Art

PROJECT: *Hope Valley Lutheran Church and Community Center*

CLIENT: *Lutheran Homes Incorporated*

SIZE: *Total area of project, 486 square feet (45 square meters)*

LOCATION: *Adelaide, South Australia, Australia*

ARCHITECT: *Matthews Architects, Adelaide*

One of two triptychs portraying the Baptism, the life of Jesus Christ, and the Resurrection. Note the use of German hand-made reamy, opal, and opak glasses and bevels.

Detail: Bright, antique glasses contrast with surrounding dense opak screened and painted border, beveled crosses, and a ribbon representing the Resurrection and promise of eternal life.

The second triptych is thematically related to music and the Miracle of Pentecost. The screen-printed music on the left and the texts on the right offer a visual link between the calligraphy in the sanctuary and the quilts at the rear.

Berin Behn and Jan Aspinall

Architectural Stained Glass Studio
312A Unley Road, Hyde Park 5061
Adelaide, South Australia, Australia
61 8 8272 3392 phone • 61 8 8272 3392 fax

Jan Aspinall and Berin Behn are South Australian-based glass artists who have collaborated in a quest to expand the horizons of contemporary stained glass and to promote its many applications in architecture. They are keen to create among architects and interior designers an awareness of the potential for incorporating glassworks in the early design stages of a project. Along with windows and doors, they have created glass for wall pieces, lift walls, screens, and office furniture.

When undertaking a project, many concerns and factors converge: the architectural concept, the function of the building, the requirements for color and light, the symbolic nature of the finished space, and any necessary heritage or appropriate historical associations or links.

Aspinall and Behn consider a significant part of their work is in achieving a balance of all these factors. Much of their combined efforts assure the glasswork harmonizes with its surroundings as an integral part of the framework of the building, yet retains a sense of artwork in itself.

Behn and Aspinall have more than twenty years combined experience and have won a number of awards, including the Royal Institute of Architects (South Australia) inaugural Art in Architecture Award in 1989, the inaugural Craft in Architecture Award of Merit (Crafts Council of South Australia and the RAIA), and an Art in Architecture Award of Merit and Commendation in 1993.

This interior overview features one side of the church from left to right, and highlights the sandblasted sanctuary windows, the dormer windows above the sanctuary, the center triptych windows, and the quilts along the back wall.

This detail of the midsection of the left-central column shows the various glasses and bevel.

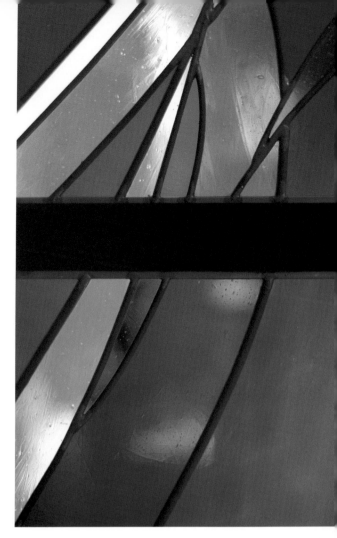

Detail highlighting the contrast between cool grey opal and colored antiq glasses.

PROJECT: *Adelaide Magistrates Court Redevelopment*

CLIENT: *Magistrates Court*

SIZE: *36 feet x 30 feet (11 meters x 9 meters)*

LOCATION: *Adelaide, South Australia, Australia*

ARCHITECT: *Denis Harrison, Building Project Management Services, S. A.*
Richard Brecknock, Brecknock Consulting

Model of project in progress. This is a major public redevelopment behind an existing historical building in the central square of Adelaide. Artwork is integrated throughout the building; the project is the gridded atrium window in the center of the photograph.

An exterior view of the window by night shows the texture of gray and clear reamy glass, clear rippled glass, and the colored, shaded borders and bands.

PROJECT: *ANZ Bank Redevelopment*

CLIENT: *Australian and New Zealand Banking Corporation*

SIZE: *33 feet x 8 feet (10 meters x 2.3 meters) plus 162 square feet (15 square meters) in same building*

LOCATION: *Gawler, South Australia, Australia*

ARCHITECT: *Swanbury Penglase Architects, Adelaide*

A view of the "link" window from the alley. Its theme refers to natural and architectural bridges, hills, rivers, and building details, and it offers privacy from the alley.

ARCHITECTURAL COMMISSIONS

Adelaide Magistrates Court
Adelaide, South Australia

ANZ bank
Gawler, South Australia

Beneficial Finance Corporation
Adelaide, South Australia

Centennial Park Cemetery Trust
Adelaide, South Australia

Church and Community Center
Lutheran Homes
Hope Valley, South Australia

Industrial Courts
Adelaide, South Australia

Our Lady of the Sacred Heart
Church and Community Center
Henley beach, South Australia

Strategic Management Services
Melbourne, Victoria

St. Andrew's Hospital
Adelaide, South Australia

Telstra Corporation
Adelaide, South Australia

AFFILIATIONS

Crafts Council of South Australia

Royal Institute of Architects, South Australia

This detail of one screen shows how the glass has been cut and arranged to create the feeling of running water in the plane of the glass.

PROJECT: *Screens*

CLIENT: *St. John's College*

SIZE: *Twenty panels, each 7¼ feet x 2 feet (2.2 meters x 0.6 meters) ten panels, each 7¼ feet x 4½ feet (2.2 meters x 1.4 meters) total area: 648 square feet (60 square meters)*

LOCATION: *New Garden Building, St. John's College, Oxford, England, U.K.*

ARCHITECT: *Richard MacCormac, MacCormac Jamieson Prichard*

Here the working of the glass has been created by setting the chance elements of the chipping process against the formality of the grid pattern.

43 Jersey Street, Hafod

Swansea, West Glamorgan SA1 2HF Wales, U.K.

44 179 246 2801 phone • 44 179 248 0281 fax

Alexander *Beleschenko*

Alexander Beleschenko started his artistic career as a painter and printmaker, disciplines that continue to underscore his approach to working with glass. Ever vigilant of being trapped by the seductive and "easy won" beauty of the material, his approach has been to create a language of harmony between glass, light, and architectural space.

Each of Beleschenko's commissions has been an exploration of not only artistic expression, but new techniques within the craft of glass making. He feels particularly privileged to be working at this juncture in time, when architecture is being constantly redefined by new materials and technologies, all of which he is keen to embrace. Beleschenko firmly believes in the importance of the artist's contribution to architecture. Within the context of a shared vision between client, architect, and artist there is a huge opportunity to push forward with new ideas.

Recently, Beleschenko's work has been developing along two distinct paths. His ambitions of bringing painting to glass still persists in his self-initiated pieces, in which all the definitions of content and context are set by him alone. His other pursuit is in developing new ways of embellishing the surfaces of industrially produced glass. Given the technology and machinery at the disposal of the glass industry, new ways of developing the language of the relationships between glass, light, and architectural space can be found and implemented. In this way, our built environment will become richer, and, hopefully, so will our daily lives.

This set of screens is made up of 60,000 pieces of glass that have been sawed and then chipped to create planes of light-capturing effects.

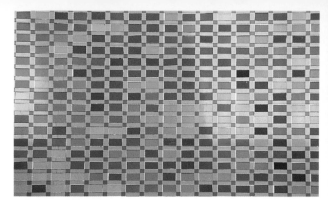

PROJECT: *"Glass Piece"*

CLIENT: *NEC Ltd /Birmingham City Council*

SIZE: *28 feet x 20 feet (8.4 meters x 6 meters); forty-two panels, each 2 feet x 7 feet (.6 meters x 2.1 meters); total area: 562 square feet (52 square meters)*

LOCATION: *Birmingham International Convention Centre, Birmingham, England, U.K.*

ARCHITECT: *Percy Thomas Partnership*

When seen at close range, each individual piece of glass is seen within the encasing grid of enameled glass.

PROJECT: *"Glass Column"*

CLIENT: *British Rail*

SIZE: *Two panels, each 2½ feet x 4½ feet (.8 meters x 1.4 meters); eight panels, each 6 feet x 4½ feet (1.8 meters x 1.4 meters) total area: 279 square feet (25.8 square meters)*

LOCATION: *Station Concourse, Reading Station Concourse, Reading, Berks, England, U.K.*

ARCHITECT: *British Rail*

Reaching up to the roof of the building, this glass and steel column has surface treatments that take advantage of the light that pours in through the glazed roof area.

PROJECT: *Gueston Hall windows*

CLIENT: *Avoncroft Museum*

SIZE: *1 foot x 2½ feet (.3 meters x .8 meters)*

LOCATION: *Gueston Hall, Avoncroft Museum of Historic Buildings, Bromsgrove, England, U.K.*

ARCHITECT: *Associated Architects*

One of eight small windows where antique glass is etched and layered to create strong visual accents within the massive constructs of the walls of the building

ARCHITECTURAL COMMISSIONS

Screen Ruskin Library
Lancaster University
England, U.K.

Windows for Avoncroft Museum
of Building
Bromsgrove
England, U.K.

Designs for glass treatments to
Cone Wall
Intermediate Concourse
Southwark Station, JLE.
England, U.K.

Windows for Galton Bridge Station
Birmingham, commissioned by
Centro
England, U.K.

Windows for Jewellery Quarter
Station
Birmingham, commissioned by
Centro
England, U.K.

Glass screens for atrium
Oxford, commissioned by St. John's
College
England, U.K.

Suspended glass panels for Church
Milton Keynes, commission by
Church of Christ the Cornerstone
England, U.K.

Windows for offices
Winchester, commissioned by
Hampshire County Architects
Department
England, U.K.

Suspended glass and steel structure
commissioned by Birmingham
International Convention Centre
England, U.K.

Interior screens
Falkirk Sheriff Court, commissioned
by the PSA
England, U.K.

Glass Column
Reading Station, commissioned by
British Rail
England, U.K.

Sculptural objects
Wimbledon Bridge, commissioned
by Speyhawk
England, U.K.

Glass banners
County Hall, commissioned by
Essex County Council
England, U.K.

Stockley Park entrance window
commissioned by Stanhope
England, U.K.

Interior screen
commissioned by Leicester Royal
Infirmary
England, U.K.

AFFILIATIONS

Royal Institute of British Architects (honorary fellow)

Royal Society of Arts (fellow)

British Society of Master Glass Painters (fellow)

PROJECT: *Stair treads*

CLIENT: *Wall Garden Hotel*

SIZE: *3 1/4 foot x 1 foot x 15 foot (1.1 meter x .3 meter x 4.5 meters) stairs*

LOCATION: *Vancouver, British Columbia, Canada*

Non-slip cast, tempered, and laminated privacy stair treads.

PROJECT: *Colored, curved cable, suspended collage*

CLIENT: *Canadian Airlines International*

SIZE: *20 feet x 5 feet (6 meters x 1.5 meters)*

LOCATION: *Toronto, Ontario, Canada*

The curved, colored collage plays off of the video terminals in the airport, while the cables allow the glass to "fly." This was Joel Berman Glass Studio's first cable project, and is one of three sculptural partitions in the Toronto airport.

Joel Berman Glass Studios Ltd.

#1-1244 Cartwright Street

Vancouver, British Columbia, Canada V6H 3R8

604 684 8332 phone • 888 505 GLASS toll-free

604 684 8373 fax

Joel *Berman*

Joel Berman feels that glass has a mystique and a refinement that can serve any metaphor, or any function. Although architects traditionally have used glass as a flat plane, Berman insists it is much more than that. As an architectural medium, it's the perfect blend of aesthetics and function. Whether transparent, translucent, or opaque, glass brings a narrative dimension to the play of light and shadow that no other material can duplicate.

Glass is a malleable material, and can be curved, textured, suspended by cables, laminated, or imbedded with crystal liquids or fiber optics. The only limits to its potential are those artists impose by restricting their imagination.

Berman, who studied at Seattle's famed Pilchuk Glass Center, has been stretching those limits since 1977. His atelier, Joel Berman Glass Studios Ltd., based in Vancouver, B.C., has been at the forefront of innovative architectural art glass since its inception in 1980. With his staff of ten artisans, Berman works closely with architects and clients to produce such dramatic site-specific elements as the floating wall for the Trump Casino in Chicago, a glass collage wall for Motown Records corporate headquarters in Los Angeles, or innovative cable-suspended, laminated-glass collages at the International Airports in Toronto and Vancouver.

With kilns capable of casting glass in sheets as large as 6 feet x 10 feet (1.8 meters x 3 meters), Berman and his staff can fabricate, shape, and texture glass for virtually any function, meeting, or exceeding any building code. Berman continues to explore new design directions and introduce new uses for glass. Most recently, he has been experimenting with stair treads made of cast non-slip safety glass, and a 90-foot (27-meter) glass bridge. Simply put, Berman wants to push glass into the twenty-first century.

PROJECT: *Curved, cast, and etched glass collage, with metal screen laminated in between glass layers*

CLIENT: *Diversey Corporation*

SIZE: *26 feet x 9 feet (7.8 meters x 2.7 meters)*

LOCATION: *Toronto, Ontario, Canada*

This abstract landscape collage curved to a 24-foot (7.2-meter) radius depicts the client's worldwide presence. "Age of Discovery" maps are subtly incorporated into the glass.

PROJECT: *Cable-suspended, recycled cast glass lobby ceiling collage, with stainless steel cables and pins*

CLIENT: *The Young Group*

SIZE: *5 feet x 9 feet (1.5 meters x 2.7 meters)*

LOCATION: *Vancouver, British Columbia, Canada*

This ceiling-suspended collage is mostly made from recycled glass. The collage plays with the entry architecture of the building.

PROJECT: *Cast abstraction of sedimentary rock to reflect gas company source*

CLIENT: *BC Gas*

SIZE: *30 feet x 9 feet (9 meters x 2.7 meters)*

LOCATION: *Vancouver, British Columbia, Canada*

The glass abstractly reflects sedimentary rock, the source of fossil fuels.

ARCHITECTURAL COMMISSIONS

Canadian Airlines International
Toronto, Ontario and Vancouver,
British Columbia, Canada

Eastman Chemical
Kingsport, Tennessee

Fleet Bank
New York, New York

Motown Records
Los Angeles, California

NAFTA Free Trade Center
Mexico City, Mexico

National City Bank
Minneapolis, Minnesota

Smed International
Vancouver, British Columbia
Calgary, Alberta, Canada
Chicago, Illinois
New York, New York

TCI
Denver, Colorado

Towers Perrin
Seattle, Washington

Wells Fargo Bank
Phoenix, Arizona

AFFILIATIONS

Glass Arts Society
British Columbia Glass Artists Association
Artists in Stained Glass

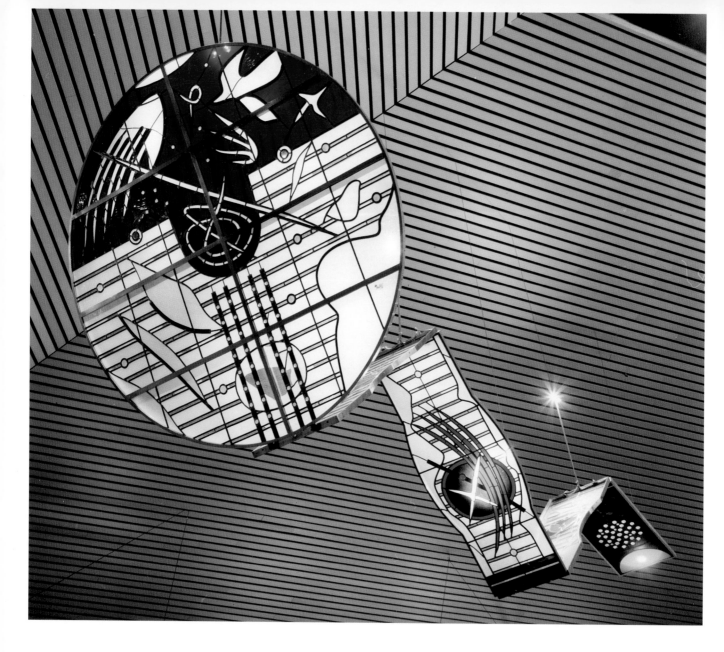

PROJECT: *"Blue Dragon"*

CLIENT: *Reykjavik Art Museum, Reykjavik Municipal Theater*

SIZE: *6 feet x 25 feet x 1½ feet (1.8 meters x 7.5 meters x .5 meters)*

LOCATION: *Reykjavik, Iceland*

ARCHITECT: *Thorsteinn Gunnarsson, Olafur Sigurdsson, Gudmundur Kr. Gudmundsson*

A free-hanging stained glass kite designed to evoke joy and happiness. A combination of opal and opaque white glass and transparent glass offer a play of graphic textures and lines. The piece can be installed in different positions.

Stained Glass Artist

Laufasvegur 52

101 Reykjavik, Iceland

354 552 2352 phone • 354 552 2354 fax

Leifur *Breidfjord*

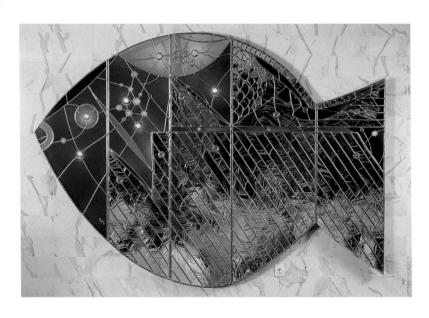

PROJECT: *"Silver from the Sea"*

CLIENT: *Engenerings Savings Bank*

SIZE: *6 feet x 9 feet (1.8 meters x 2.7 meters)*

LOCATION: *Reykjavik, Iceland*

ARCHITECT: *Johann Asmundsson*

The goldfish design features opal and transparent glass in conjunction with mirrored antique glass. The halogen light bulbs can be changed by taking away the prisms.

When creating an artwork of stained glass, four aspects of light have to be taken into account: Stained glasswork seen from inside the building during daylight, inside after dusk, outside the building in daylight, and outside in the evening.

Breidfjord already has a lifetime's worth of projects under his belt. His stained glass windows, both large and small, can be found in almost two dozen churches all over Iceland, as well as in churches in Germany and Scotland. St. Giles' in Edinburgh, the cathedral of Scottish Protestants, is perhaps the most famous example of his work. Another dozen of his windows grace banks, schools, and other public buildings in Iceland, including two architectural landmarks of recent origin: the National Library building and the newly inaugurated Supreme Court building. Recently, Breidfjord was commissioned to execute a stained glass window for a Reykjavik building of political rather than architectural consequence. The joint Anglo-German Embassy building is the only one of its kind in the world. Breidfjord also has provided his share of stained glass windows for private houses and collectors.

Two free-hanging stained glass kites designed to harmonize with the frame structure of the architecture. Opal and opaque glass are used in contrast with transparent glass.

PROJECT: "Yearning for Flight"

CLIENT: Leifur Eriksson International Airport

SIZE: 24 feet x 32 feet (7.2 meters x 9.7 meters) and
16 feet x 32 feet (4.8 meters x 9.7 meters)

LOCATION: Keflavik, Iceland

ARCHITECT: Gardar Halldorsson

PROJECT: "The Human Spirit: Past–Present–Future"

CLIENT: National and University Library of Iceland

SIZE: 7¼ feet x 20½ feet (2.2 meters x 6.2 meters)

LOCATION: Reykjavik, Iceland

ARCHITECT: Mannfred Vilhjalmsson

This work depicts three heads. The one on the left represents the past, with text from old Icelandic manuscripts. The center one shows the present, with text under a computer sign. The one on the right shows the future, an unwritten sheet.

PROJECT: *"Flags"*

CLIENT: *British Embassy and German Embassy*

SIZE: *6 feet x 16 feet (1.8 meters x 4.8 meters)*

LOCATION: *Reykjavik, Iceland*

ARCHITECT: *Olafur Sigudsson*

The outside view of this window is as important as the inside view. The window is made of mostly opaque glass and opal-opaque white glass shading into clear glass. It shows free interpretation of the British flag on one side, with the German flag on the other. The Icelandic flag ties them together. The yellow stars from the European flag are scattered liberally throughout.

PROJECT: *"Med Logum Skal Land Byggja"*

CLIENT: *Supreme Court of Iceland*

SIZE: *5 1/4 feet x 32 feet (1.6 meters x 9.6 meters)*

LOCATION: *Reykjavik, Iceland*

A commission of stained glass for the Supreme Court of Iceland to harmonize with the curved lines of the architecture of the building. An experiment with bending a stained glass art work to achieve sculptural effects. The text is an old law text featuring Breidfjord's own calligraphy.

ARCHITECTURAL COMMISSIONS

British Embassy, German Embassy
Reykjavik, Iceland
Architect: Olafur Sigursson

City Hall
Eruption Memorial Window
Vestmannaeyjar, Iceland
Architect: Gudjón Samúelsson

Fossvogschapel
Reykjavik, Iceland
Architect: Olafur Sigurdsson

Grensáschurch
Reykjavik, Iceland
Architect: Jósep Reynis

Katholische Kirche
Steibis, Germany

Leifur Eriksson International Airport
Keflavik, Iceland
Architect: Gardar Halldórsson

National Bank of Iceland
Neskaupstadur, Iceland
Architect: Hróbjartur Hróbjatrson

P. Bröste A/S
Copenhagen, Denmark

St. Giles' Cathedral
Robert Burns Memorial Window
Edinburgh, Scotland, U.K.
Architect: James Simpson

Supreme Court
Reykjavik, Iceland
Architects: Margrét Hardardóttir,
Steve Christer

AFFILIATIONS

Félagi í Félagi íslenskra myndlistarmmanna

Félagi í Sambandi íslenskra myndlistarmanna

Félagi í British Master Glasspainters Society

PROJECT: *Church windows*

CLIENT: *Catholic Church*

LOCATION: *Blumenthal/Eifel*

(right and opposite page)

PROJECT: *Church windows*

CLIENT: *Catholic Church St. Peter*

LOCATION: *Recklinghausen, Germany*

Execution by Derix, Taunusstein, Germany.

Obermassener Kirchweg 16a

59423 Unna, Germany

49 2303 12842 phone • 49 2303 12842 fax

Wilhelm *Buschulte*

Born in 1923 in Massen, Germany, Wilhelm Buschulte studied at the Academy of Fine Arts in Munich, where he was Meisterschüler, a student of special distinction. The winner of numerous prizes and competitions, Buschulte is considered one of the primary figures in the German postwar art glass movement. His work has been exhibited worldwide, at the Arte Liturgica in Rome, the Sacred Art Exhibition in Minneapolis, the Weltausstellung Bruxelles, the Art Sacré Contemporain in Paris, as well as at exhibitions in Malaga, Sevilla, Valencia, Lisbon, Bombay, and Ars Sacra Cologne.

PROJECT: *Window for exhibition and concert room*

CLIENT: *English Church*

LOCATION: *Bad Homburg, Germany*

Window in the English Church, which was newly created for exhibition and concert purposes. Execution by Derix, Taunusstein, Germany.

The crypt window is made of slab glass and glass bars.
Execution in 1983.

PROJECT: *Church windows*

CLIENT: *Church of St. Gereon*

LOCATION: *Cologne, Germany*

St. Ursula, painting on glass. Execution in 1983 by Oidtmann,
Mönchengladbach, Germany.

ARCHITECTURAL COMMISSIONS

Cathedral
Aachen, Germany

Church Maria im Kapitol, Crypt
Cologne, Germany

Seminary for priest
Cologne, Germany

St. Gereon
Cologne, Germany

St. Heribert
Cologne, Germany

St. Paul's Cathedral
Frankfurt, Germany

Seminary for Priest
Paderborn, Germany

Cathedral
Ratzeburg, Germany

German Embassy
Riyadh, Saudi Arabia

Reformation Memorial-Church
Worms, Germany

PROJECT: *"Hanging Garden"*

CLIENT: *Culver City*

SIZE: *28 feet x 24 feet (8.4 meters x 7.2 meters)*

LOCATION: *City Hall, Culver City, California*

ARCHITECT: *C.H.C.G. Architects, Pasadena, California*

*Involving three offset screens, the artwork serves to inte-
grate and graphically focus elements of the building's
facade. Its forms descend from the roof line in a geometric
abstraction, suggesting a hanging garden in bloom.*

1812 NW 24th Avenue

Portland, Oregon 97210

503 224 6729 phone • 503 241 3142 fax

Ed *Carpenter*

Ed Carpenter brings to his monumental glass commissions a keen architectural sensitivity and a singular ability to introduce lyrical and mysterious elements into potentially arid architectural contexts. The grandson of a painter and sculptor and stepson of an architect, he combines their influences into a unique approach to his own art.

Having worked on public and corporate commissions for twenty-five years and completed more than fifty in the United States and abroad, his experience has prepared him for solving a wide variety of problems. His solutions frequently result in such technical innovations as his use of cold-bent tempered glass and suspension of laminated glass on cables. He is known equally, however, for his willing collaborative spirit and his sensitivity to the atmospheric needs of a space.

Many of Carpenter's installations contain a puzzling dualism. They are simultaneously biological and engineered, or traditional and technological, creating an ambivalent relationship to their surroundings. Are they growing out of the walls, flying within the space, or constructed for some scientific purpose? This ambiguity increases his work's metaphoric power and provokes sustained interest in the viewer.

Attention is also held by Carpenter's manipulation of sunlight through the use of mirrors, lenses, and reflective glasses. He frequently treats buildings as giant periscopes and his sculptures as enormous phototropic organisms, leaving one wondering where the building ends and the art begins.

PROJECT: *Meydenbauer Convention Center*

CLIENT: *Bellevue, Washington Parks Department*

SIZE: *25 feet x 25 feet x 8 feet (7.5 meters x 7.5 meters x 2.3 meters), fountain and sculpture; 60 feet x 49 feet x 8 feet, (18 meters x 15 meters x 2.3 meters), lobby sculpture*

LOCATION: *Bellevue, Washington*

ARCHITECTS: *Kohn Pederson Fox, New York, New York H.N.T.B., Bellevue, Washington*

This installation greets users of the convention center as they approach, and gives a celebratory spirit to the building. Daylight produces a moving canvas of colored projections and shadows within the center. At night, programmed lighting plays off the piece, creating a subtly changing series of enormous "light paintings" on both the inside and outside walls.

PROJECT: *Morgan Library, Colorado State University*

CLIENT: *Colorado Council on the Arts*

SIZE: *56 feet x 60 feet x 22 feet (17 meters x 18 meters x 6.5 meters)*

LOCATION: *Ft. Collins, Colorado*

ARCHITECT: *LOA Architects, Denver, Colorado*

Rooted in the building and ascending with it toward the sunlight, this installation reinforces the architecture while adding a dynamic, lyrical element. As light symbolizes knowledge, both the sculpture and the library reach out to it.

PROJECT: *Oakland Federal Building*

CLIENT: *General Services Administration*

SIZE: *Approximately 1000 square feet (90 square meters)*

LOCATION: *Oakland, California*

ARCHITECT: *K.M.D., San Francisco, California*

The design was developed to graphically integrate with the rotunda architecture while providing colorful highlights inside and outside, in both day and night. When direct sunlight strikes the glass, a brilliant array of brightly colored moving projections fills the rotunda.

ARCHITECTURAL COMMISSIONS

Bellevue Convention Center
Bellevue, Washington

Broward Community College
Fort Lauderdale, Florida

City Hall
Culver City, California

City Hall Plaza Tower
Orlando, Florida

Federal Building
Oakland, California

Morgan Library
Colorado State University
Fort Collins, Colorado

1251 Rockefeller Center
New York, New York

Red Cross College
Akita, Japan

St. Mark's Cathedral
Seattle, Washington

University of Wisconsin
School of Business Administration
Madison, Wisconsin

PROJECT: *CTS Structural Glass Prisms*

CLIENT: *Irwin Management Company, Inc.*

SIZE: *30 feet x 10 feet x 2 feet (9 meters x 3 meters x .6 meters)*

LOCATION: *Indianapolis, Indiana*

ARCHITECTS: *Edward Larrabee, Barnes & Associates*

These structural glass windows, created for the Christian Theological Seminary's chapel, reflect and transmit color and patterns of natural light into the high space.

(opposite page) The colors change as light moves into the room from the southwest, from noon to sunset, tracking a subtle and complicated path through the space.

James Carpenter Design Associates, Inc.

145 Hudson Street

New York, New York 10013

212 431 4318 phone • 212 431 4425 fax

James *Carpenter*

The work of James Carpenter focuses on the exploration of light and its influence within architecture and the environment. In using glass as a mediator of light, Carpenter's work has led to an intensive technical exploration of it as a structural element. He has invented methods of attachment, such as tensile systems, and expanded the properties of glass so that it takes on a presence of its own within a defined environment. Since 1979, Carpenter and senior members of his studio have exploited the phenomenon of light afforded by the properties of glass: transparency, reflectivity, and compressive strength. With a rich knowledge of both the technical and aesthetic aspects of glass, Carpenter creates dynamic environments and spaces through the integration of specific elements: walls, windows, bridges, and sculptures. His work often crosses the traditional boundaries between architecture, engineering, and fine arts.

Carpenter's studio is a collaborative organization that encourages an interchange of ideas and design responsibilities between Carpenter and studio architects Luke Lowings, Janet Fink, Richard Kress, and Rebecca Uss, as well as material and structural engineers and fabricators. Often working in association with engineers and other architectural offices, Carpenter has completed a multitude of significant building projects and public art commissions. He is currently focusing on large-scale projects, including a series of pedestrian bridges, a synagogue designed with a cast glass facade, and the creation of a dramatic urban site within the redevelopment of the Central Artery Tunnel in Boston, Massachusetts.

PROJECT: *Refractive glass wall*

CLIENT: *First Hawaiian Bank, The Myers Corporation*

SIZE: *98 feet x 48 feet x 26 feet (30 meters x 14 meters x 7.8 meters)*

LOCATION: *Honolulu, Hawaii*

ARCHITECT: *Kohn, Pedersen & Fox*

The refractive glass wall prevents direct light from entering the lobby/exhibition space and reveals the changing characteristics of the unique Hawaiian sunlight.

Parallel to the clear exterior skin is a secondary layer of diffused, etched glass which acts as a projection screen for the patterns of light refracted through the glass prisms.

This glass climate-barrier is comprised of a vertical structural system of laminated glass prisms, post-tensioned against one another and standing just inside of a clear exterior glass skin.

The stair is suspended from the ceiling with a central tapered conical net of stainless steel rods stiffened by tensioning against the lower floor.

PROJECT: *Tension net stair*

CLIENT: *Private*

SIZE: *23 feet x 10 feet (7 meters x 3 meters) diameter*

LOCATION: *Chicago, Illinois*

ARCHITECT: *Larson Associates Inc., Chicago*

View from the mezzanine of this spiral glass staircase suspended from a tensioned, tapered, conical column.

ARCHITECTURAL COMMISSIONS

BMW AG
Munich Airport, Germany

Christian Theological Seminary
Indianapolis, Indiana

First Hawaiian Bank
Honolulu, Hawaii

German Foreign Ministry
Berlin, Germany

Hong Kong Landmark Property
Hong Kong

Massachusetts Highway Department
Boston, Massachusetts

Millenium Partnership
New York, New York

Mississippi River Bridge
City of Saint Paul, Minnesota

Pedestrian Bridges
City of Bremerhaven, Germany

Portland Center for Performing Arts
Portland, Oregon

San Francisco International Airport
San Francisco, California

AFFILIATIONS

American Institute of Architects, Associate (AIA)
American Society of Civil Engineers, Affiliate (ASCE)
Society of Glass Technology, UK
Illuminating Engineering Society of North America (IESNA)
International Solar Energy Society (ISES)

The two 35-foot (10-meter) glass towers consist of seventeen spans of curved, carved, and colored glass 10 feet x 2 feet x ¾ inches (3 meters x .6 meter x 2 centimeters). Each of the 1,800 pound stainless steel columns is fastened with 18-inch (46-centimeter) bolts to steel plates located beneath the floor.

PROJECT: *Twin carved glass towers*

CLIENT: *Investors Group*

SIZE: *Each tower 35 feet x 12 feet x 1½ feet (10 meters x 3.6 meters x .5 meter)*

LOCATION: *One Canada Center, Winnipeg, Manitoba, Canada*

ARCHITECT: *Webb Zerafa Menkes Housden Partnership*

"Prairie Boy's Dream" continued an area of fascination for Carther that began with the Canadian Embassy: aerial views of patterns in the earth created by farmers.

PROJECT: *Carved glass wall, Canadian Embassy*

CLIENT: *Canadian Government/Shimizu Corporation/Mitsubishi Bank*

SIZE: *25 feet x 22 feet (7.5 meters x 6.5 meters)*

LOCATION: *Tokyo, Japan*

ARCHITECT: *Moriyama and Teshima Architects*

This work takes much of its inspiration from the Japanese art of Ikebana. The composition contains various symbols in which Carther refers to Ikebana's three essential elements: heaven, man, and earth.

(opposite page)
The artist during installation. The steel support structure located at the rear of the glass is just visible. The structure was designed to cause the least visual interference and to resist most earth tremors.

Carther Studio, Inc.

464 Hargrave Street

Winnipeg, Manitoba, Canada R3A 0X5

204 956 1615 phone • 204 942 1434 fax

Warren *Carther*

One of the first things you notice when viewing Warren Carther's work is the scale of many of his pieces, their mass, the thickness of the glass, and the depth of the carving. He takes advantage of the structural capabilities of glass to create works that, at times, appear to defy gravity, as in the curved and carved glass towers of "Prairie Boy's Dream." The carved glass wall for the Canadian Embassy in Tokyo, with its 91 panels, has no mullions cluttering the work; rather each panel is surrounded by air. The support structure is located at the rear. The only hints of the method of structural support are the squares of stainless steel visible at the corners of each panel.

Carther began his exploration of glass as a glass blower at a small art school in upstate New York in 1974. After a few years and more glass blowing at the California College of Arts and Crafts, he understood that the kind of scale that excited him was not possible at the end of a blow pipe. This, combined with a deeply felt love of architecture, led him to develop his current methods of working in glass.

Carther believes that experiencing art in a public space during the course of one's day can be a highly rewarding and enriching experience. From the earliest of times, most societies have had some form of art accessible to its people. Carther wonders if, by tucking away so much of our art in museums, we are losing something essential in our daily lives.

Carther continues to be fascinated with the unique physical properties of glass. It can be transparent, translucent, and opaque. Glass gives the artist the ability to control light, an essential element in both art and architecture. It connects the two in a way no other material can.

PROJECT: *Carved glass wall*

CLIENT: *Manitoba Lotteries Corporation*

SIZE: *26 feet x 11 feet (7.8 meters x 3.2 meters)*

LOCATION: *Winnipeg, Manitoba, Canada*

ARCHITECT: *Don Courtnage, Courtnage and Company*

This curved and carved ³/₄-inch-thick (2-cm-thick) glass wall is airbrush painted, and some of the color is achieved with dichroic glass laminations. Its thematic inspiration was the gaming industry, but the usual symbols were deliberately avoided to allow for a more individual expression.

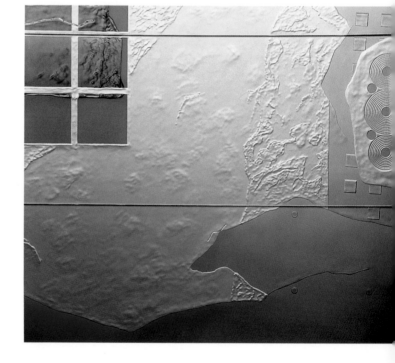

PROJECT: *Entry piece*

CLIENT: *Private residence*

SIZE: *11 feet x 9 feet (3.2 meters x 2.7 meters)*

LOCATION: *Winnipeg, Manitoba, Canada*

ARCHITECT: *Gilbart Architectural Design*

Free-standing entry piece for residence. Carved and painted glass with cast aluminum support structure.

PROJECT: *"Scribe With Pet Sculpin"*

CLIENT: *Murray Simkin, Private residence*

SIZE: *7 feet x 6 feet (2.1 meters x 1.8 meters)*

LOCATION: *Winnipeg, Manitoba, Canada*

ARCHITECT: *Lloyd Secter Architects*

The support structure was the prototype for the vastly larger scaled Canadian Embassy project.

ARCHITECTURAL COMMISSIONS

Canadian Embassy
Tokyo, Japan

Investors Group
Winnipeg, Manitoba, Canada

Legislative Assembly Building
Yellow Knife, Northwest Territories,
Canada

Manitoba Lotteries Corp.
Winnipeg, Manitoba, Canada

AFFILIATIONS

Ontario Association of Architects

California College of Arts & Crafts (BFA, glass)

Naples Mill School of Arts & Crafts (Studio Glass Studies, hot glass)

University of Manitoba (Undergraduate studies in Fine Art)

There are glasses of great volume and relief that accentuate the main points in the most dramatic areas.

PROJECT: *"Ciencia Y Naturaleza"*

CLIENT: *Bayer Labs*

SIZE: *24 panels, 4 feet x 10 feet (1.4 meters x 3 meters) each*

LOCATION: *Barcelona, Spain*

ARCHITECT: *Elisenda Tortajada, Mambar Studio*

This project embraced the seven floors of an office building. The apparently abstract composition symbolizes nature and science. There are both organic and geometric forms represented in the piece. The organic elements are free shapes that refer to water, soil, and plants. The geometric shapes refer to chemistry, as well as systematic and Cartesian scientific investigation.

(opposite page)

PROJECT: *"Naturaleza Mito Y Geometria"*

LOCATION: *León, Spain*

ARCHITECT: *Antoni Gaudí*

Mallorca 330

08037 Barcelona, Spain

34 3 207 3302 telephone • 34 3 459 2057 fax

José Fernández *Castrillo*

José Fernández Castrillo is a creator of glass art designed to work with large scale forms adapted to the spaces of modern architecture. His contributions to the history of the stained-glass window are demonstrated through "vitrographies," glass panels on which he seems to paint with light—not on the glass, but in the glass.

Castrillo was born in a little town close to León in northern Spain, but he has spent most of his life in Barcelona, where he has had the chance of developing his work in optimal cultural surroundings. He has always had a fascination with glass, and although his first solo exhibition wasn't until 1984, he realized his first work as a glass artist when he was nineteen years old. Since that moment he has been exploring different techniques, traveling in an interior world, discovering more facets of this material on a daily basis.

Castrillo refers to himself as a glass nomad, deliberately attempting to go further, to take his creative work to the limit of the unexplored. By using gentle lines, or by mistreating the glass, he has managed to provide the medium with new techniques as well as to express his own lyrical, poetic, and passionate world. His work always produces something identifiable that harmonizes with its surroundings.

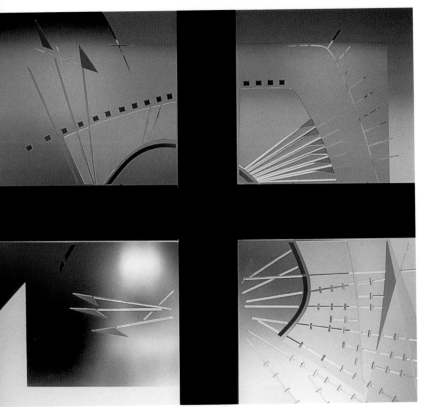

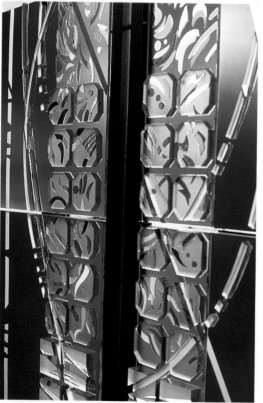

PROJECT: *"Barcelona Olimpica"*

CLIENT: *Barcelona City Hall and Santa Maria del Mar Cathedral*

SIZE: *23 feet x 4 feet (7 meters x 1.2 meters)*

LOCATION: *Barcelona, Spain*

ARCHITECTS: *Berenguer de Montagut, ca. 1330*
Aureli Santos, 1995 (partial restoration)

The main color is blue to relate to the sea, and the structure tries to be quite respectful of gothic stained glass. There is a central area where things are explained and where most of the symbols are situated. The areas on both sides are simply ornamental. The vitrography commemorates the Olympic games in Barcelona in 1992, but its symbolism mostly refers to the Olympic city itself.

PROJECT: *"Al Vent"*

CLIENT: *Mr. and Mrs. Verges*

SIZE: *6¹⁄₂ feet x 15 feet*
(2 meters x 4.5 meters)

LOCATION: *Malgrat de Mar, Spain*

The dominant blue color refers to the Mediterranean residential setting. The composition was inspired by a cloth waving in the wind.

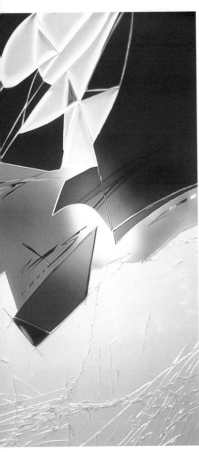

PROJECT: *"Entidad Fuera de Contexto"*

CLIENT: *Dr. Walter Henry and*
Mrs. Maria del Carmen Calvo

SIZE: *2¹⁄₂ feet x 1¹⁄₂ feet*
(0.8 meter x 0.5 meter)

LOCATION: *Laguna Beach, California*

Here, the ideas of Duchamp, Miro, or Picasso about converting found objects to pieces of art is realized in glass. The broken laminar glass gives the composition great character, strength, and contrast.

PROJECT: *The Victoria Quarter*

CLIENT: *Prudential Assurance*

SIZE: *8,000 square feet (743 square meters)*

LOCATION: *Leeds, England*

ARCHITECT FOR RENOVATION: *Derek Latham & Company*

Brian Clarke was asked to contribute a proposal for a stained glass artwork to accompany the renovation of Queen Victoria Street in the center of Leeds, a street designed by theater architect Sir Frank Matcham and built in the nineteenth century.

In collaboration with renovation architects Derek Latham & Company, Clarke designed and fabricated a 400-foot-long (120-meter-long) colored rooflight that spans the existing street from end to end. The composition is the largest single work of stained glass in Great Britain. To allow plenty of natural daylight into the street and to reduce the amount of colored light falling on the already polychromatic tiling of Matcham's architecture, clear glazing was inserted where the eaves of the modern roof meet the Edwardian street facade. Visitors to the Victoria Quarter are treated to an unforgettable colored sky, which even on grey autumn afternoons, enlivens the space.

Toni Shafrazi Gallery

119 Wooster Street

New York, New York 10012

212 274 9300 phone • 212 334 9499 fax

TSGallery@aol.com e-mail

Brian *Clarke*

English-born artist Brian Clarke is acknowledged as one of the world leaders in architectural art. And although glass art is his primary artistic forum, he has not restricted his creative output solely to architectural commissions. His paintings, stained glass, mosaic, and tapestry works can be found in both architectural settings and private and public collections throughout the world.

His largest project to date, a recently completed shopping center in Rio de Janeiro, is illustrated here together with a smaller, though equally startling installation in southern Italy.

Clarke's previously completed architectural works include collaborations with architects Sir Norman Foster, Will Alsop, Arata Isozaki, Future Systems, Zaha Hàdid, and Skidmore, Owings, and Merrill. In these commissions, he has displayed an unparalleled understanding and sensitivity toward the built environment and its integration with art.

Clarke executed the world's largest stage sets for the 1993 Paul McCartney New World Tour. Additional clients have included Pfizer Pharmaceuticals, the Swiss Bank Corporation, and the Abbaye de la Fille Dieu in Romont, Switzerland. In his art, Clarke expresses an insatiable appetite to collaborate at the highest level.

Clarke is a visiting professor of Architectural Art at University College London and an Honorary Fellow of the Royal Institute of British Architects. His work is represented by the Tony Shafrazi Gallery in New York.

PROJECT: *Norte Shopping Center*

CLIENT: *Engenharia, Comercio e Industria S.A.*

SIZE: *Stained glass: 11,356 square feet (1,055 square meters); mosaic: 1,572 square feet (146 square meters)*

LOCATION: *Rio de Janeiro, Brazil*

ARCHITECT: *Luis Carlos Pereira de Azevedo, Lindi, Brazil*

(top left)
The grand court of the Norte Shopping center is the focal point of the entire complex. A ring of mosaic interacts with the central stained glass skylight. The motif of ribbons uses bits of text, the words of which borrow from colloquial expressions of Carnival. The ribbon weaves and twists into both the mosaic and the stained glass.

(top right)
The stained glass and mosaic of the grand court as viewed from directly below.

(bottom left)
Another view down the principal mall showing the rooflight.

PROJECT: *Valentino Village*

LOCATION: *Noci, Bari, Italy*

In this design, pools of light fall onto the floor of the conference theater and mute the inside room. The glass acts as a screen to the strong Mediterranean sunlight, and by virtue of the light coming through the glass, the room is animated by fragments of color.

At night, illuminated from within, the window forms a curved, radiant, colored frieze.

PROJECT: *Didcot Library*

CLIENT: *Oxford County Council*

SIZE: *4 feet (1.2 meters)*

LOCATION: *Oxford, England, U.K.*

ARCHITECT: *Oxford City Council*

The round window is made of traditional leaded glass with painting, staining, and acid etching. It is in the children's library and contains images of children's faces and figures working on repairing trains at the adjacent railway museum.

(opposite page)

PROJECT: *Glass canopy*

CLIENT: *Middlesbrough Council*

SIZE: *33 feet x 23 feet (10 meters x 7 meters)*

LOCATION: *Middlesbrough, England, U.K.*

DESIGNER: *Martin Donlin*

In a national competition to design a canopy/meeting place for city dwellers, glass is suspended on steel wires, and is toughened and enameled. Middlesbrough is a historic steel town in the north of England, and the design makes reference to Vulcan, the god of fire and forge.

16 St. Catherine's

Wimborne Minster

Dorset BH21 1BE England, U.K.

44 120 284 9321 phone • 44 120 284 9321 fax

Martin *Donlin*

All of Martin Donlin's projects are slightly different, so it is difficult to assign to him a standard approach. Although the work is contemporary in its feel, Donlin relies upon the tradition of storytelling in his glass work, using both classical figures and abstract, representational images. As architecture once used classical images to adorn its buildings, Donlin makes reference to the purpose and use of a building through the use of images and text on glass.

Architectural artwork can play different roles through the use of image, form, and text. It can relate to the physical characteristics and location of a site. It can refer to the historical heritage and meaning of a site. It can act as a marker establishing an identity of a site, creating a sense of place. It can be relevant and accessible to the users of a site. Often, the artwork is intended simply to create a site-specific atmosphere or ambiance.

Donlin studied architectural glass at Swansea in the artist craftsman tradition. However, his recent projects have become much larger in scale, so collaboration with glass studios in Britain and Germany has become essential. Donlin works closely with architects to ensure a harmonious link between his glasswork and the structure and function of a building.

Techniques that characterize Martin's work are deep sandblasting and acid polishing of float glass, traditional leaded glass, and, more recently, large sheets of enameled toughened glass that complement contemporary architectural glazing systems. Some of his current projects include such techniques as large-scale casting and bending of glass.

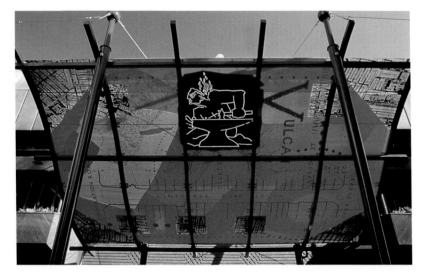

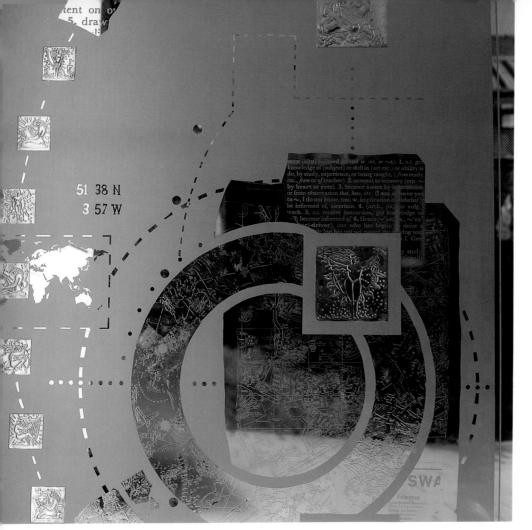

PROJECT: *Swansea University*

CLIENT: *Swansea University*

SIZE: *8 feet x 5 feet (2.3 meters x 1.5 meters)*

LOCATION: *Swansea, Wales, U.K.*

ARCHITECT: *Percy Thomas Partnership*

This is a detail of an entrance screen containing acid etching and polishing. The design contains "the seven liberal arts" as a reference to the Swansea Institute of Learning.

PROJECT: *Forum Center*

CLIENT: *Chester City Council*

SIZE: *20 feet x 16½ feet (6 meters x 5 meters)*

LOCATION: *Chester, England, U.K.*

ARCHITECT: *Leslie Jones Partnership*

The design reveals the classical image of Ceres. The glass is sand-blasted and flush-fitted into the specially designed Pilkington Planar Glazing System.

PROJECT: *Euston House*

CLIENT: *Euston House*

SIZE: *10 feet x 10 feet (3 meters x 3 meters)*

LOCATION: *Euston, London, England, U.K.*

ARCHITECT: *Euston House*

This screen appears to be free-standing. In fact, the glass disappears below ground and is bolted to a steel plate 8 inches (20 centimeters) below the marble.

PROJECT: *M.A.F.F. (Ministry of Agriculture, Fisheries, and Food)*

CLIENT: *H.M. Government of England*

SIZE: *10 feet x 7 feet (3 meters x 2.1 meters)*

LOCATION: *York, England, U.K.*

ARCHITECT: *R.M.J.M., London, England, U.K.*

This window for the new M.A.F.F. building refers to a bird's eye view of agricultural forms and botanical growth. It also includes the abstracted forms of Flora and Zephyr in glass paint.

ARCHITECTURAL COMMISSIONS

B.B.C.
Wales
Cardiff, England, U.K.

Broadgate Club
London, England, U.K.

Espress Club
London, England, U.K.

Euston House
Euston, London, England, U.K.

Forum Center
Chester, England, U.K.

MAFF
Yorkshire, England, U.K.

Middlesbrough Council
Middlesbrough, England, U.K.

Pfizer UK
Sandwich, Kent, England, U.K.

Sir Terence Conran
Butler's Wharf
London, England, U.K.

Sunderland City Library and
Art Gallery
Sunderland, England, U.K.

Swansea University
Wales, England, U.K.

YMCA
Manchester, England, U.K.

AFFILIATIONS

Architectural Glass, Swansea, England, U.K. (training)
Livermead Art Glass, London, England, U.K.
Nero Glass, London, England, U.K. (studio)
T&W IDE, London, England, U.K. (studio)
Solaglass, Bradford, England, U.K. (studio)
Colin Telford, Wales, England, U.K. (studio)

PROJECT: *"Espiral"*

CLIENT: *Private Residence, "Casa Malintzin"*

SIZE: *18 feet (5.5 meters)*

LOCATION: *Mexico City, Mexico*

ARCHITECT: *Eduardo Dyer*

Twenty-four panels, suspended from steel cables at different angles, form a helicoidal spiral, bathing a patio with bright, colored, and slowly moving images.

(opposite page)

PROJECT: *"El Vidrio en el Espacio y en el Tiempo"*

CLIENT: *Sílices de Veracruz, S.A. de C.V.*

SIZE: *10 feet x 10 feet x 10 feet x 36 feet (3 meters x 3 meters x 3 meters x 11 meters)*

LOCATION: *Orizaba, Veracruz, Mexico*

ARCHITECT: *Corporación Bajel, S.A. de C.V.*

STAINLESS STEEL STRUCTURE: *Servi-Estructuras Alfa, S.A. de C.V.*

Morelia Glass Design Center

Apartado Postal No. 670

58000 Morelia

Michoacàn, Mexico

52 4 323 1280 phone • 52 4 323 1280 fax

Bert *Glauner*

From his early youth, Bert Glauner's interests lay in art—or whatever looked like it. Against his family's stern resistance, he studied painting, jewelry design, and sculpture. Only vehement pressure from his father persuaded him to enter the family business and run a jewelry company. After long years in an industrial environment, he was introduced to glass artistry by a good friend from Boston.

Glauner feels that a strong, aesthetic design concept forms the basis for successful work in the field. He sees his creations as an integral part of the tectonic space; a symbiosis between space and light, enhanced and modulated by glass.

After all these years of playing with leaded stained glass he has experimented with new techniques of lamination and chemical bonding, opening up a whole new language of expression. Above all, what concerns him, and what he seeks to explore through his work, is the magical, the mysterious, and the sensual.

To commemorate the inauguration of a new furnace, this leading manufacturer of glass containers commissioned the artist to design and fabricate an allusive monument to glass.

PROJECT: *Glass mural for Board of Directors room*

CLIENT: *Banca Serfin, S.A.*

SIZE: *23 feet x 7¹/₄ feet (7 meters x 2.2 meters)*

LOCATION: *Mexico City, Mexico*

ARCHITECT: *Estudio J. Lóyzaga, S.A. de C.V., Edmundo Pérez Toledo*

Framed by a stainless steel structure, ten panels form a glass mural of laminated safety and mouth-blown antique glass, bevels, and sand carving.

The half-view of the glass mural features sunlit bevels, accentuating shades of gray and blue patches of opal antique glass.

PROJECT: *Room divider*

CLIENT: *Estafeta Mexicana, S.A. de C.V.*

SIZE: *20 feet x 7¹/₄ feet (6 meters x 2.2 meters)*

LOCATION: *Cuernavaca, Morelos, Mexico*

ARCHITECT: *Eduardo Dyer*

Six laminated panels divide the director's office from reception area. The divider is constructed with sandwiched handmade bark paper, and is supported by a roughly polished steel structure.

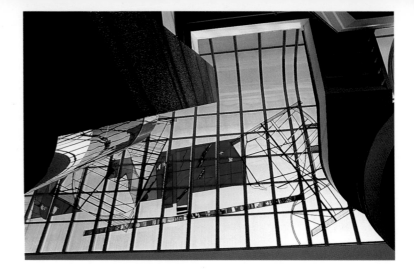

PROJECT: *Installation for polycarbonate-covered patio roof*

SIZE: *63 feet x 30 feet (19 meters x 9 meters), hanging at 45-degree angle under roof*

LOCATION: *Morelia, Michoacán, Mexico*

ARCHITECT: *Fernando Pérez Córdoba*

"Enigmas del Sacbé Perdido" is framed by an elevator shaft and sculpted staircase.

PROJECT: *Window for staircase*

CLIENT: *Banca Serfin, S.A.*

SIZE: *4¼ feet x 12½ feet (1.4 meters x 3.8 meters)*

LOCATION: *Mérida, Yucatán, Mexico*

ARCHITECTS: *Ernesto Nataren, Pablo Caso, Agustín Paulino, Mauricio Mendoza, and Antonio Mondragón*

A design for the restoration of a beautiful turn-of-the-century mansion. The idea here is the juxtaposition of different styles; an original venetian-crystal chandelier hangs in front of the window.

ARCHITECTURAL COMMISSIONS

"Caminos de Michoacán"
Zirahuén, Michoacán, Mexico

Grupo Cail
Mexico City, Mexico

Hotel San Cayetano
Zitácuaro, Michoacán, Mexico

Houseboat, Harry D. Page
Sausalito, California

Residencia Grimm
Tepoztlán, Morelos, Mexico

Residencia Sada González
Mexico City, Mexico

Residencia Such
Mexico City, Mexico

Residencia Ugarte
San Sebastián, Spain

Templo El Corazón de María
Morelia, Michoacán, Mexico

Torre Acuario
Mexico City, Mexico

AFFILIATIONS

Asociación de Artistas Vidrio, A.C. (AAV, founding member)
Mexico City, Mexico

PROJECT: *Windows for all choir chapels*

CLIENT: *Cathedral Maria-Empfängnis*

SIZE: *27 feet high (8.2 meters high)*

LOCATION: *Linz, Austria*

The image shows the design for two of the twelve windows.

OJECT: *Windows in the north and south transept*

CLIENT: *Catholic Church St. Martinus*

SIZE: *32 feet high (9.6 meters high)*

ATION: *Greven, Westfalen, Germany*

mage shows the window of the south transept. The glass is ...erts opal and leaded antique.

(opposite page)

PROJECT: *Window for the western choir*

CLIENT: *Bamberg Cathedral*

SIZE: *15 feet high (4.5 meters high)*

LOCATION: *Bamberg, Germany*

The glass is Lamberts opal and leaded antique. In this late Romanesque-Gothic cathedral, the graphic representation shows a so-called "three-jet event" from nuclear physics. The red panels are separated in front of the window.

Parkstrasse 97

D-65191 Wiesbaden, Germany

49 611 956 6119 phone • 49 611 956 6170 fax

Karl-Martin *Hartmann*

Karl-Martin Hartmann studied biology at the University of Mainz, and received his degree as a microbiologist. He then went on to study art at the Hochschule für Bildende Künste-Städelschule in Frankfurt, and since 1985 has worked as a freelance artist.

Hartmann feels that art is necessary for a society, that, in this day and age, is able to think in global terms. Art is the complementary pole to the reality of life that is determined by functionalism. An artist who works for the public sphere is obliged to express his views on contemporary topics through his work.

Hartmann wants to reach people with his work. He wants to motivate them by stimulating pensiveness and emotional perception through the senses. His goal is to cause intellectual reflection, to stimulate people to reflect upon their own views of topical issues.

PROJECT: *Free-standing sculptures of steel and glass*

CLIENT: *JVA-Weiterstadt*

SIZE: *10¼ feet high (3.1 meters high)*

LOCATION: *Darmstadt-Weiterstadt, Germany*

Frame of galvanized steel, doubled Antique glass with rolled lead enclosed in safety glass. The image shows the design for five of thirteen objects. The commission will be executed in the early summer, 1997.

PROJECT: *Free-standing objects*

CLIENT: *Catholic Church Maria-Aufnahme*

SIZE: *Up to 8½ feet high (2.5 meters high)*

LOCATION: *Wiesbaden, Germany*

ARCHITECT: *Rudi Studer, Zürich, Switzerland*

Frames of galvanized steel, doubled antique glass with rolled lead enclosed in safety glass. The image shows six of the twelve objects.

PROJECT: *Free-standing sculpture of steel and glass within the exhibition "L'Harmonie des Verres"*

SIZE: *26 feet high (7.8 meters high)*

LOCATION: *Chartres, France*

Frame of galvanized steel, doubled antique glass with rolled lead enclosed in safety glass.

PROJECT: *Glass sculptures*

CLIENT: *District court*

SIZE: *29 feet (8.8 meters), 6¼ feet (1.9 meters), and 8¼ feet high (2.4 meters high)*

LOCATION: *Bad Hersfeld, Germany*

ARCHITECT: *Ulrich Gräber, Darmstadt, Germany*

A large object in front of a huge glass wall. The antique glass is held by plastic crosses and enclosed in safety glass. Two smaller objects are enclosed in the insulation glass.

ARCHITECTURAL COMMISSIONS

Bad Hersfeld District Court

Berlin competition "Denkmal für die ermordeten Juden"

Chartres free-standing sculpture out of steel and glass "Stele"

Dessau-Klieken free standing sculpture out of steel and glass "Stele"

Gerleve/Westfalen Benedict Monastery

Köln Catholic Church of St. Peter

Linz/Austria windows for all choir chapels in the cathedral

Project for the nave-windows of the Regensburg Cathedral

Speyer overall plan for the cathedral

Weiterstadt, the prison chapel

Partial interior view of the prayer hall at night.

Outside view of one window.

PROJECT: *Islamic Ornamentation*

CLIENT: *Burnaby Jamatkhana*

SIZE: *Eight three-dimensional windows in prayer hall, each 16 feet x 8 feet (4.8 meters x 2.3 meters)*

LOCATION: *Burnaby, British Columbia, Canada*

FABRICATED BY: *Hein Derix Glasstudios, Kevelaer, Germany*

ARCHITECT: *Bruno Freschi Architects, Vancouver, Canada and Buffalo, New York*

Interior view of a window during daylight.

1461 Nelson Avenue

West Vancouver, British Columbia,

Canada V7T 2G9

604 926 8594 phone • 604 926 9452 fax

Lutz *Haufschild*

Lutz Haufschild is one of Canada's most respected artists working with glass and light. His thoughtful integration of art and architecture has resulted in over two hundred commissions in Canada, Europe, Japan, and the United States.

Haufschild is captivated by the shaping of natural light and considers light his true medium. Site-specific requirements inspire creativity in him. Accordingly, his artistic response to architectural givens is often bold, using strong colors. At other times, when appropriate, his work is restrained, with clear glasses, bevels, and prisms creating a timeless elegance. He believes that as we shape our buildings, the buildings in turn shape us.

Architect, critic, and glass artist Ken vonRoenn has written the following about Haufschild's work: "neither his art nor the architecture is encumbered or diminished by the other, rather the appreciation of both is heightened by their relationship."

Haufschild's innovative fabrication methods and sensitive aesthetic treatments combine to create harmonious and distinct work. His more notable public projects include the majestic "Great Wave Wall" at the Vancouver International Airport, a piece that measures over 131 feet (40 meters) in length; the three-dimensional cast glass windows at the Burnaby Jamatkhana (Ismaili Prayerhouse); the bas relief "Tribute to Baseball" at the Skydome Stadium in Toronto; the subtle "Spectra Veil" at Bata Shoe Museum in Toronto; and the exuberant windows depicting the Four Seasons at St. Mary's Church in Vancouver.

Haufschild has taught and lectured in many countries. He has been the recipient of numerous awards, including the coveted Saidye Bronfman Award in 1988. Haufschild was elected to the Royal Canadian Academy of Arts in 1995.

Detail of silverstained cast glass.

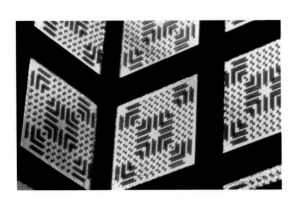

PROJECT: *"The Trinity Windows"*

CLIENT: *St. Andrew's Lutheran Church*

SIZE: *Thirty windows, more the 1200 square feet (106 square meters)*

LOCATION: *Toronto, Ontario, Canada*

FABRICATED BY: *Derix Glasstudios, Taunusstein, Germany*

"God the Father" window with a reflection of the "God the Holy Spirit" window.

PROJECT: *"The Great Wave"*

CLIENT: *Vancouver International Airport, International Arrival and Departure Concourse*

SIZE: *28 feet x 131 feet (8.5 meters x 40 meters)*

LOCATION: *Vancouver, British Columbia, Canada*

FABRICATED BY: *Kits Glass Company, Richmond, British Columbia, Canada*

ARCHITECT: *Waisman Dewar Grout Carter Architects, Vancouver, Canada*

Thousands of pieces of tinted float glass were cut into 1-inch (2.5-centimeter) wide strips. These are then stacked so that their diverse and radiant edges can take full advantage of any and all light, making the art glass appear in a sensuous luminosity.

PROJECT: *"The Four Seasons"*

CLIENT: *St. Mary's Parish Church*

SIZE: *6 feet x 32 feet (1.8 meters x 10 meters)*

LOCATION: *Vancouver, British Columbia, Canada*

FABRICATED BY: *Kits Glass Company, Richmond, British Columbia, Canada*

ARCHITECT: *Dalla Lana Griffin Architects, Vancouver, British Columbia, Canada*

"Winter" window, with the reflection of "Summer."

PROJECT: *"The Spectra Veil"*

CLIENT: *Bata Shoe Museum*

SIZE: *45 feet x 35 feet (13.5 meters x 10 meters)*

LOCATION: *Toronto, Canada*

FABRICATED BY: *Kits Glass Company, Vancouver, British Columbia, Canada*

ARCHITECT: *Moriyama and Teshima Architects, Toronto, Canada*

Detail with cantilevered staircase.

ARCHITECTURAL COMMISSIONS

Bata Shoe Museum
Toronto, Ontario, Canada

Burnaby Jamatkhana
Vancouver, British Columbia, Canada

Canada Trust
Toronto, Ontario, Canada

East 21 Hotel
Tokyo, Japan

Civic Center Fire Station
Lynnwood, Washington

Skydome Stadium
Toronto, Ontario, Canada

St. Mary's Parish Church
Vancouver, British Columbia, Canada

Telesat Canada
Ottawa, Ontario, Canada

Vancouver International Airport
Vancouver, British Columbia, Canada

Villa Chatour Lamin
Vevey, Switzerland

Westminster Abbey Church
Mission, British Columbia, Canada

AFFILIATIONS

Royal Canadian Academy of Arts (RCA, elected member)
Artist in Stained Glass (past president)
International Guild of Glass Artists, Inc. (board member)

PROJECT: *Stanford Biomedical Center*

CLIENT: *Stanford University*

LOCATION: *Palo Alto, California*

ARCHITECT: *Stone Marraccini Patterson Architects*

This is the project for which Huether developed the INNER-LITE® technique. Challenged by SMP Architects to create a new decorative glass compatible with the stringent requirements of contemporary building technologies, AGD developed INNER-LITE® to combine thermal insulating, safety glazing, colored decorative glass, and sand-etching within an insulating glass window.

PROJECT: *Boardroom*

CLIENT: *Oracle Corporation*

LOCATION: *San Francisco, California*

ARCHITECT: *Seccombe Design Associates*

Standard tenant improvement aluminum window walls were upgraded by including dual glazed INNER-LITE® decorative glass in this conference room.

(opposite page)

PROJECT: *Lincoln Plaza Cafeteria*

CLIENT: *Pers/Lincoln Plaza Office Building*

SIZE: *60 feet x 5 feet (18 meters x 1.5 meters)*

LOCATION: *Sacramento, California*

ARCHITECT: *LPA Architects*

Sand-etched "icons" create a playful texture counterbalanced by a large expanse of green, mouth-blown glass, which recalls the deep color of the agricultural land surrounding the state capital.

Architectural Glass Design

101 South Coombs Street, Suite X

Napa, California 94559

707 255 5954 phone • 707 255 5991 fax

Gordon *Huether*

Gordon Huether's work in glass has always been a collaboration of sorts: A collaboration between the client (the architectural community), his team at Architectural Glass Design, and a strong sense of relevance to those who will be using the space on a daily basis.

Huether always tries to approach every project with no preconceived notions as to what techniques or artistic content might be employed. This allows him the freedom to push the envelope in the medium of glass.

This attitude led Architectural Glass Design to the development of one technique in particular that has allowed them to offer the architectural community an alternative to traditional art glass solutions. Huether's firm was fortunate enough to receive a patent for this technique, known as INNER-LITE®. INNER-LITE® incorporates two or three layers of glass with laminated colored or textured glasses with etching on the adjoining layers. These layers are then sealed in a thermally insulated unit.

This technique takes advantage of a unique and dynamic interplay of color, light, and shadow. It is through this new technique that Huether finds himself doing projects all over the world, from hospitals to airports to museums to private homes.

Huether believes that rather than becoming a lost art, stained glass is becoming a fine art. He uses stained glass primarily as a tool for personal artistic expression.

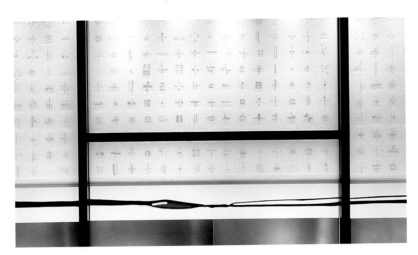

PROJECT: *Mt. Timpanogos Mormon Temple*

CLIENT: *The Church of Latter-Day Saints*

SIZE: *5,000 square feet (450 square meters)*

LOCATION: *American Fork, Utah*

Here Huether developed architecturally sympathetic design concepts with the thermal and structural capabilities of INNER-LITE®. The design included over 1,500 mouth-blown rondels and over 12,000 square feet (1,080 square meters) of treated glass surface. The Mormon Church has said of the project that "AGD's work simultaneously solved several problems by spanning across vision and spandrel areas without interrupting the continuity of the design."

PROJECT: *Meditation room*

CLIENT: *University of California, San Diego*

SIZE: *15 feet x 10 feet (4.5 meters x 3 meters)*

LOCATION: *San Diego, California*

ARCHITECT: *Carmen Farnum Igonda Design*

The sculpted leaded glass screen for UCSD Meditation Room won the 1994 AIA Design Award for Religious Art in Architecture. The work expresses the primal elements of earth, water, and fire brought together in a spiritual environment without the use of traditional symbolism.

PROJECT: *Lobby*

CLIENT: *Oracle Corporation*

LOCATION: *Redwood City, California*

ARCHITECTS: *Seccombe Design Associates, Gensler and Associates*

Designed in collaboration with Christine Stone, the lobby of Oracle Corporation's headquarters features decorative glass for five towers that wind their way through the spaces. The towers recall the movement of the tide in the nearby San Francisco Bay.

ARCHITECTURAL COMMISSIONS

Church of Jesus Christ of Latter-Day Saints
Utah, Hong Kong, Philippines

Dominican Sisters
San Rafael, California

Getty Center
Los Angeles, California
Architect: Richard Meier & Partners

Hiroshige Museum of Art
Tendo, Japan

Houston Lighting and Power
Houston, Texas
Architect: DMJM Keating

Kaiser Hospital
Sacramento, California
Architect: Dreyfuss & Blackford Architects

Methodist Hospital
Sacramento, California
Architect: Nacht & Lewis Architects

Mulia Group
Jakarta, Indonesia
Architect: HOK Architects

National Airport
Washington, D.C.
Architect: Cesar Pelli & Associates

University of Alaska
Fairbanks, Alaska

PROJECT: *Westminster Abbey*
Poets Corner

CLIENT: *Westminster Abbey*

SIZE: *324 square feet (30 square meters)*

LOCATION: *London, England, U.K.*

ARCHITECT: *Christopher Wren*

Poets' Corner is one of the most visited sites in England. This memorial to the poets of Great Britain is a modern response to a historical setting. The window is built in the traditional style.

(opposite page)
This detail shows the complexity of technique: triple etching, three applications of paint, and plating of glass. Only through this uncompromising process can the emotion of glass color be achieved.

58 First Avenue

London SW14 8SR England, U.K.

44 181 876 6930 phone • 44 181 876 6930 fax

Graham *Jones*

Graham Jones, for many years predicted as the leading exponent in the younger generation of this medium, has now achieved an international reputation with a list of some thirty major commissions.

His work spans the architectural divide from medieval Westminster Abbey to the Far Eastern Tower in Shanghai, China of Lucky Target Square. Yet throughout this variety of work, Jones constantly strives for the original response that each commission should elicit. This, he believes, is the great challenge of architectural art.

Although early in his career Jones was acknowledged as a gifted colorist, his work can swing, if dictated by the building, to the purist transparency and white of suspended flat glass walls. Such is the case in his 864-square-foot (80-square-meter), three-story entrance screen for Smith Klein Beecham Headquarters in Harlow, England. Here a cloud vortex in painted washes of etched glass is interspersed with minimal stripes of color, the drama strong but not overwhelming.

The challenge of the Westminster Abbey commission became a personal crusade for Jones. Contemporary art can inhabit any setting; here, the easy option would have been a non-statement or an egotistical, uncompromising slight on the historical setting. Jones, however, chose a strong, richly colored approach, taking quotations of style from the period to ease the transition into the Abbey's milieu. The result has been applauded by the critics.

His love of glass and his insistence that art must not be dictated by the medium has led him to push the boundaries of convention with the great glass workshops of Europe. Yet beneath all the technical processes in Jones' work lies the soul of an emotive painter.

PROJECT: *Minster Court*

CLIENT: *Prudential Properties*

SIZE: *5 feet (1.5 meters)*

LOCATION: *London, England, U.K.*

ARCHITECT: *G.M.W. Partnership*

This suspended glass sculpture adds drama to the main entrance of a London trading center.

PROJECT: *Stockport Shopping Mall*

CLIENT: *Hamerson Group*

SIZE: *600 square feet (180 square meters)*

LOCATION: *Stockport, England, U.K.*

ARCHITECT: *BDP Manchester*

This series of eighteen windows is a progression of color balance for both sides of a shopping arcade. A laminated glass process gives a collage effect.

PROJECT: *Main entrance screen*

CLIENT: *Smith Klein Beecham Headquarters*

SIZE: *864 square feet (80 square meters)*

LOCATION: *Harlow, England, U.K.*

ARCHITECT: *A.M.E.C. and the Hillier Group*

To screen meeting rooms from the main entrance lobby, sixty-three etched, tempered glass panels, laminated with pieces of antique glass, were suspended from yacht masts using a bolting system.

PROJECT: *Colmore Gate Office Complex*

CLIENT: *Church Commissioners England*

SIZE: *864 square feet (80 square meters)*

LOCATION: *Birmingham, England, U.K.*

ARCHITECT: *Seymore Harris*

This is the central section of a project that is wrapped around half of the ground floor of the entrance to the building. The main purpose of this abstract landscape is to semi-obscure the exterior walkway.

ARCHITECTURAL COMMISSIONS

Coca Cola Headquarters
London, England, U.K.

ICI Corporate Headquarters
London, England, U.K.

Lucky Target Square Hospital
Shanghai, China

Prudential Developments Office
Complex
Berkeley Square
London, England, U.K.

Shell Oil UK Ltd
ShellMex House
London, England, U.K.

PROJECT: *Medical office lobby*

CLIENT: *Kaiser Permanente*

SIZE: *13 feet x 32 feet (4 meters x 9.6 meters)*

LOCATION: *Napa, California*

ARCHITECT: *E. Paul Kelly Berkeley, California*

The large circular forms represent a single cell that, incredibly, has the innate ability to reproduce itself. This unique characteristic to recreate new life through the miracle of independent functioning rouses images of new meaning from one of the most basic forms we know—the circle. Rebirth, reproduction, healing, resurrection, life beyond death, spirituality, unlimited power, higher self, heaven on earth, eternity, the world, and the universe are all represented here.

(opposite page)

PROJECT: *Kaiser medical facility*

SIZE: *8 feet x 10 feet (2.3 meters x 3 meters)*

LOCATION: *San Francisco, California*

ARCHITECT: *Hospital Designers Inc., St. Louis, Missouri*

Through the effective use of mirrors, prisms, lenses, and colored handblown glass, imaginative optical illusions of depth and layered light results. Crossing Kaiser's threshold, Jurs's work momentarily elevates thought and alleviates stress. Patients feel at once vital and tranquil.

Jurs Architectural Glass

4167 Wilshire Boulevard

Oakland, California 94602

510 521 7765 phone • 510 531 6173 fax

Shelley *Jurs*

Shelley Jurs completed her formal education at the University of California in Santa Barbara and the College of Arts and Crafts in Oakland, California. She trained in architectural glass techniques at the Cummings Studios in San Rafael, California, and at the Swansea College of Art in South Wales, Great Britain. She continued her formal apprenticeship training at the Willets Stained Glass studios in Philadelphia, became a personal assistant to Ludwig Schaffrath in Germany, and later returned to the United States to start her own successful business.

Jurs believes the art of glass is an articulation of the dance with life. Her careful choice of clear-faceted prisms, dimensional spheres, and transparent, translucent, and iridescent textures combines to

express optical illusions of depth and layered light. The materials become a reflective expression of the belief that life is defined by light. Jurs's work imports a feeling of the inner spirit as well as a sense of time-lessness. Her method of glass design intoxicates through the richness of material and simplicity of its artistic expression.

As we are now faced with the question of communi-cation of urban art and architecture, it becomes essential that art operates in response to the building as a meaningful and well-integrated statement. Their mutual roles serve a psychological purpose, which can lead to a metaphorical interpretation. In this way, integrating art and architecture has the ability to function as something that stimulates response and becomes a condition of the thought process. The two become dependent for their existence, value, and significance.

Architectural glass as art triggers a response that embraces both nature and human life. It offers a positive emotional effect for those who celebrate it.

PROJECT: *Front entry*

CLIENT: *Private residence*

SIZE: *3 feet x 8 feet (1 meter x 2.3 meters)*

LOCATION: *Castro Valley, California*

PROJECT: *Diamond Heights*

CLIENT: *Private residence*

LOCATION: *San Francisco, California*

This piece is fashioned after the idea of a Japanese shoji screen. Absorbent prismatic glass, rather than paper, comprises the partition. This glass screen allows translucent light to pass between the spaces more freely, fracturing imagery with faceted surfaces.

PROJECT: *La Coquille Club*

CLIENT: *Lobby of condominium complex*

SIZE: *22 feet (6.5 meters) in diameter*

LOCATION: *Florida*

ARCHITECT: *Interactive Resources, Richmond, California*

Celestial and stellar phenomena allude to the sky and suggest heaven, astrophysics, eternal and universal life. Color is created through the use of no color; nature touching humanity with beams of light.

PROJECT: *Civic Center*

CLIENT: *City of Oceanside and the Mayor's Office*

SIZE: *21 feet x 12 feet (6.4 meters x 3.6 meters)*

LOCATION: *Oceanside, California*

ARCHITECT: *Charles Moore, UIG, Los Angeles, California; Robbin Hayne Design, Malibu, California*

"Pyramid Power" recalls the ancient belief that the pyramid will bring you closer to heaven. It is a reminder that secular environments can become sacred places, and that a temporal experience can elevate our thought process in a meeting place where government policy affects public life.

PROJECT: *Public Library*

CLIENT: *Friends of the Library*

SIZE: *12 feet x 8 feet (3.6 meters x 2.3 meters)*

LOCATION: *Redwood City, California*

ARCHITECT: *Ripley Associates, Phylis Martin Vegue*

A simple, ordered, elegant, and systematically arranged glass motif lends reference to the essential order of the interior space. Subtle modern graphics make use of strong geometric shapes. The emphasis is on the symmetrical with an asymmetrical twist. The glass lends insight and makes a connection between the building's historic entry to its contemporary interior counterpart.

ARCHITECTURAL COMMISSIONS

All Saints Chapel
Hayward, California

Catholic Church
Eshweiler, Rohe, Germany

Davis Police Station
Davis, California

Larkspur Library
Larkspur, California

Osh Kosh Correctional Facility
Osh Kosh, Wisconsin

Redwood City Library
Redwood City, California

School for the Deaf and Blind
Colorado Springs, Colorado

Shane Elliott Jewelers
Costa Mesa, California

Spring Hill Elementary School
Library
Anchorage, Alaska

University of Alaska
Auke Bay, Alaska

Color detail.

Interior view.

Main exterior view.

PROJECT: *"The Planet's Awakening"*

CLIENT: *Caja Madrid*

SIZE: *83 feet x 72 feet (25 meters x 22 meters)*

LOCATION: *Barcelona, Spain*

ARCHITECTS: *Fargas and Associates*

C/ Consejo de Ciento 111 bj.

08015 Barcelona, Spain

34 3 423 1133 phone • 34 3 423 1664 fax

Keshava

Antonio Sainz

Keshava is the artistic name of Antonio Sainz, who was born in Logroño, Spain, and studied architecture at Navarra University. After practicing as an architect, he went to Barcelona in 1983 to work in stained glass. Keshava's singularity is his first profession; he is an architect who specializes in glass art installations. Architectural elements such as facades, roofs, stairs, or interior divisions projected in glass are the areas that he works in naturally.

Keshava manages a professional team of other architects, engineers, economists, and artisans, who collaborate to resolve special structural problems with light, adding artistic value to a building. The focus of his work begins with a comprehension and interpretation of the architectural space, with the knowledge that it is possible to serve architecture with his artistic work in glass. Keshava brings imagination and an architectural sensibility to his studies of how light influences interior spaces. The result is artwork that not only displays a technical solution to a problem, but also distinguishes a building with its chromatics, symbolism, and philosophical meaning. He is always testing new techniques for making stained glass, looking for the best expression of a given composition in colorized glass.

In addition to his numerous visits to artists' studios, factories, and schools of glass, Keshava has studied with such important glass artitsts as Ludwig Schaffrath, Johannes Schreiter, Ed Carpenter, and Narcissus Quagliata, among others.

View of moving sculpture, "The Permanent Eclipse," with "The Planet's Awakening" window in the background.

PROJECT: *"The Permanent Eclipse"*

CLIENT: *Caja Madrid*

SIZE: *15³/₄ feet (4.8 meters) in diameter*

LOCATION: *Barcelona, Spain*

ARCHITECTS: *Fargas and Associates*

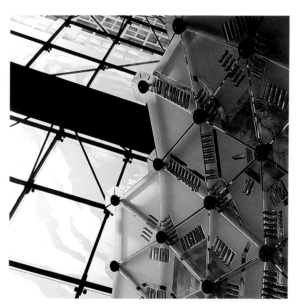

Detail of moving sculpture.

PROJECT: *"Sun Lantern" for a staircase*

CLIENT: *Architectural office building*

SIZE: *11 feet x 7½ feet x 9 feet (3.3 meters x 2.3 meters x 2.7 meters)*

LOCATION: *Barcelona, Spain*

ARCHITECT: *Antonio Caramés*

This structure consists of five glass panes and opens onto a terrace from a stairwell. The vertical lines that form the pyramids symbolize the end of the vertical ascension.

ARCHITECTURAL COMMISSIONS

Auditorium
Capellades
Barcelona, Spain

Central Market
Logroño
La Rioja, Spain

Enologic Station Wine Cellar
Haro
La Rioja, Spain

Larrion Restaurant
Estalla
Navarra, Spain

Marqués de Murrieta Wine Cellar
Logroño
La Rioja, Spain

Office Building
Barcelona, Spain

Office Building
Logroño
La Rioja, Spain

St. Cosme & St. Damián Church
Soncillo
Burgos, Spain

Sabadell Restaurant
Barcelona, Spain

Treasury Delegation Office
Logroño
La Rioja, Spain

AFFILIATIONS

Centre International du Vitrail, Chartres, France
Designing Group of the Promotion Arts, BCN
Barcelona Glass Center Foundation, BCN
Cultural Promotion Association, BCN

Window triptych.

PROJECT: *St. Markus Church*

CLIENT: *Pastor Theodor Jordans*

LOCATION: *Bedburg, Germany*

ARCHITECT: *Trude Cornelius, Bonn, Germany*

Lower part of the angel window, 1965.

(opposite page)

PROJECT: *St. Adelheid, Geldern*

CLIENT: *Pastor Norbert Hoffacker*

LOCATION: *Geldern, Germany*

ARCHITECT: *Prof. Josef Ehren, Geldern-Veert, Germany*

Altar window, 1967, whose theme is the equality of human life. The circular graphic follows the design of a cross-section of a tree trunk.

Buchenweg 13

41334 Nettetal-Schaag, Germany

49 2153 70836 phone • 49 2153 70836 fax

Joachim Klos

Born in Weida/Thüringen, Germany, Joachim Klos studied at the state high school for architecture and fine arts in Weimar, where Professor Martin Domke was leading the foundation course in the meaning of Bauhaus. He continued his studies in Krefeld, in the department of stained glass and mosaic at the Technical Training College Niederrhein. One of his first commissions was the nave windows for the Gothic church in Mönchengladbach, Germany. In the forty years since then, Klos has been a stained glass designer, graphic designer, and color designer in the field of architecture.

Joachim Klos's work can be understood in the context of a Hugo Rahner treatise about the "playing human." According to Plato, the human being is a "living toy," not just a figure in the game, thrown around or put away by an unknown power and temper. He is built in a logistical way, an object of godlike artistic joy. And therefore, as Plato says, the best of him is to be playful: a human being who lightly, beautifully, and seriously in the fullness of confirmation, imitates the power of creation, as much as it is given to him.

PROJECT: *St. Martin Church, Veert*

CLIENT: *Pastor Josef Janssen*

LOCATION: *Veert near Geldern, Germany*

ARCHITECT: *Prof. Ehren, Geldern, Germany*

Addition of an octagon.

PROJECT: *Church Christ Our Peace, Duisburg*

CLIENT: *Pastor Günter Becker*

LOCATION: *Duisburg-Meiderich, Germany*

ARCHITECT: *Prof. Hannes Hermanns, Kleve, Germany*

Section of choir window.

ARCHITECTURAL COMMISSIONS

Christ Our Peace Church
Duisburg, Germany

Holy Ghost Church
Essen, Germany

Kreissparkasse
Schwäbisch-Gmünd, Germany

Police Academy
Hiltrup, Germany

St. Adelheid Church
Geldern, Germany

St. Antonius Church
Kevelar, Germany

St. Barnabas Church
Niedermormter, Germany

St. Markus Church
Bedburg, Germany

St. Martin Church
Veert, Germany

St. Nikolaus Church
Walbeck, Germany

Telekom Building
Osnabrück, Germany

PROJECT: *Police Academy, Hiltrup*

CLIENT: *The state of Nordrhein-Westfalen*

LOCATION: *Mübster-Hiltrup, Germany*

ARCHITECT: *Board of Works, Münster, Germany*

Glass front at the entrance hall.

PROJECT: *Kiln-formed glass wall*

CLIENT: *Brunswick Corporation*

SIZE: *9 feet x 28 feet (3 meters x 8.5 meters)*

LOCATION: *Lake Forest, Illinois*

ARCHITECT: *VOA, Chicago, Illinois*

The main wall in a corporate lobby depicts the motion and fluidity of water. The assorted patterns and artifacts sprinkled throughout the glass seem to shimmer off the glass and across the marble floor. Its color constantly changes, depending on the position of the viewer and the shifting light.

PROJECT: *Six kiln-formed glass screens*

CLIENT: *United Airlines*

SIZE: *Six screens, each 16 feet x 2 feet (4.8 meters x .6 meter)*

LOCATION: *Washington, D.C.*

ARCHITECT: *JPJ Architects, Dallas, Texas*

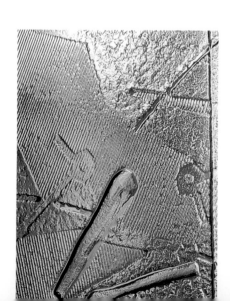

These screens were needed to provide privacy, yet let the maximum amount of light into the space. The designs are a subtle interpretation of fabric used in the space, translated into glass.

74 Commodore Road

Worcester, Massachusetts 01602

508 757 2507 phone • 508 797 3228 fax

Stephen *Knapp*

Stephen Knapp has long been on the vanguard of architectural art. Internationally renowned for his collaborative, large-scale works of art in public, corporate, and private collections, he has been instrumental in developing new techniques and materials for public art, working in a diversity of mediums, including kiln-formed, etched, cast and dichroic glass, metal, stone, mosaic, and ceramic.

With twenty-five years of experience working with architects and designers, the collaborative process has been a major focus of Knapp's work. Problem-solving, technological innovation in a wide variety of materials, and an understanding of the architect's desire for the space, are hallmarks of his work. The interchange of ideas and inspiration, and the resulting synergy that both architect and artist bring, often leads to a solution that neither would have achieved individually.

Knapp researches materials and history for the appropriate site specific pieces, melding today's technologies and resources with hints of the past. Long intrigued by the marriage of art and technology, he uses factories and fabricators as his tools, often refining the processes and developing new techniques, so his vision can become reality.

By kiln-forming glass, Knapp adds texture and dimension to glass, making it the perfect carrier for color and light, capturing them on the surface in a kinetic, changing dance of light and motion. With its ability to take and mold shapes, kiln-formed glass is also an exquisite medium for storytelling, framing metaphor in its very being.

Knapp continues to explore new uses for glass in architectural settings, combining it with marble for the Royal Caribbean Cruise Lines, and creating a dichroic glass and stainless steel bird sculpture for Harnischfeger Industries to complement his kiln-formed glass walls there. His work in sculpture, furniture, and lighting all serve as fertile ground for his architectural glass projects.

Knapp frequently lectures on architectural art glass, the collaborative process, and the integration of art and architecture.

PROJECT: Tempered, kiln-formed glass and carved marble focal wall

CLIENT: Royal Caribbean Cruise Lines, Splendour of the Seas

SIZE: 43 feet x 4¹/₁ feet x 2 feet (13 meters x 1.4 meters x .6 meter)

ARCHITECT: Arkitekbyran AB, Goteborg, Sweden

"Fragments of Time–The Explorer's Legacy" depicts Greek and Roman sailors and exploration. Working closely with the architect's theme, the glass was rough-cut to look like a broken fragment, then kiln-formed to add detail. Faces and hieroglyphics were carved into marble pieces that were then slotted to accept the glass.

PROJECT: Entry wall of tempered, kiln-formed glass

CLIENT: Harnischfeger Industries

SIZE: 9 feet x 12 feet (2.7 meters x 3.6 meters)

LOCATION: Milwaukee, Wisconsin

ARCHITECT: Kahler-Slater, Milwaukee, Wisconsin

The entry to the chairman's office needed to be a fluid, dynamic design. Because the wall would not have the side lighting of a double wall, various patterns were created to accept the light differently.

PROJECT: *Two adjacent walls of tempered, kiln-formed glass*

CLIENT: *Harnischfeger Industries*

SIZE: *9 feet x 44 feet (2.7 meters x 13 meters)*

LOCATION: *Milwaukee, Wisconsin*

ARCHITECT: *Kahler-Slater, Milwaukee, Wisconsin*

A dramatic location on Lake Michigan, with changing light and weather, plays an important part in these walls. The strong patterns in the glass are an abstract interpretation of the corporation, weaving different elements throughout. Here, dawn's golden light acts in warm contrast to the adjacent walls.

ARCHITECTURAL COMMISSIONS

Allmerica Financial Headquarters
Worcester, Massachusetts

Brunswick Corporation
Lake Forest, Illinois

California Grill
Disney's Contemporary Resort
Lake Buena Vista, Florida

CNA Insurance Companies
Chicago, Illinois

Hamilton County Justice Complex
Cincinnati, Ohio

Harnischfeger Industries
Milwaukee, Wisconsin

Lotus Development Corporation
Cambridge, Massachusetts

McDonnell Douglas
Long Beach, California

Menorah Medical Center
Kansas City, Missouri

The Quarasan Group
Chicago, Illinois

Rhapsody of the Seas
Royal Caribbean Cruise Lines

The Spa at the Heritage
Boston, Massachusetts

Splendour of the Seas
Royal Caribbean Cruise Lines

Sprint
Washington, D.C.

United Airlines
Benito Juarez International Airport
Mexico City, Mexico
Dulles Airport
Washington D.C.

USAA Federal Savings Bank
San Antonio, Texas

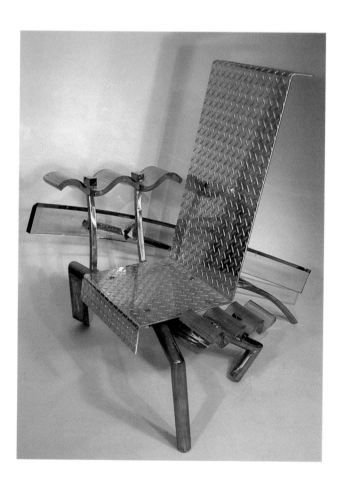

(top)

PROJECT:	*Linear wall form series*
CLIENT:	*Baldwin Development*
SIZE:	*4 panels, each 8 feet x 10 feet x 2 feet (2.3 meters x 3 meters x .6 meter)*
LOCATION:	*San Diego, California*

One-inch-thick (2.5-cm-thick) long glass strips bent into undulating linear elements and arcing lines, all backed by reflective 3/8-inch (1-cm) fumed gray glass. As you walk through the lobby you are flanked on both sides by the recessed wall sculptures.

(left)

PROJECT:	*LFF-2-95/2*
CLIENT:	*Los Angeles County Museum of Art*
SIZE:	*3 feet x 3 feet x 4 feet (1 meter x 1 meter x 1.2 meters)*
LOCATION:	*Los Angeles, California*

One-inch-thick (2.5-cm-thick) glass, with welded, brushed, sandblasted stainless steel, and a formed aluminum diamond plate seat. The chair was acquired by the Los Angeles County Museum of Art for its permanent collection during the 1995 exhibition "Common Forms, High Art."

10954 Independence Avenue

Chatsworth, California 91311

818 718 7569 phone • 818 718 2601 fax

John Gilbert *Luebtow*

John Gilbert Luebtow has been working in the architectural scale art world since 1969, when he began creating ceramic murals. This work was accomplished during his tenure as Director of the Architectural Ceramics Department at "De Porcelyne Fles" in Delft, Netherlands. His interest in glass was aroused during a collaborative exhibition with Leerdam Glass in Amsterdam.

In 1971 Luebtow returned to the United States and began exploring all aspects of glass artistry: blowing, cutting, polishing, bending, and enameling. In the process, he always strove for ways to expand his ideas and the scale of glass art into the architectural venue. After considerable experimentation and technical exploration, Luebtow designed and built his own furnaces to enable him to forge his art on a much larger scale. By the late 1970s he was able to manipulate 10-foot (3-meter) sheets of 1-inch-thick (2.5-cm-thick) glass into the undulating linear forms that have become one of the trademarks of his work.

Other materials emphasized in Luebtow's work are ceramics, metal (primarily stainless steel), and stone. These elements have been selected not only for what they bring visually to the work, but also because of their permanence, ease of maintenance, and structural integrity.

Luebtow views art in architecture as a permanent commitment, as a cultural reference that we leave for future generations. He feels that the integration of art into architecture must be birthed and nurtured with extreme sensitivity and caution in order for it to be successful. Art both influences and conditions the way the environment is perceived and received. One needs to be supportive of the other. The site and the art being equal, the sum of their parts must create a greater whole.

PROJECT: *Linear fountain*

CLIENT: *Barker Patrinely*

SIZE: *7 feet x 45 feet x 5 feet (2.1 meters x 13.5 meters x 1.5 meters); Reflecting pool: 12 feet x 12 feet (3.6 meters x 3.6 meters)*

LOCATION: *San Francisco, California*

ARCHITECT: *Skidmore, Owings, and Merrill*

The visual and auditory aspects of water accompanied by the physical and visual properties of slumped and etched 1-inch-thick (2.5-cm-thick) glass, and lighting, all set on a stage of Urazuba granite.

PROJECT: *"Invenire"*

CLIENT: *The Scripps Research Institute, Arnold and Mabel Beckman Center for the Chemical Sciences*

SIZE: *11 feet x 40 feet x 8 feet (3.2 meters x 12 meters x 2.3 meters)*

LOCATION: *La Jolla, California*

ARCHITECT: *Tucker-Sadler and Associates*

Twelve geometric shapes of 1-inch-thick (2.5-cm-thick) slumped glass with ⅕-inch (.5-cm) etched lines whose overlapping patterns define more geometric shapes, further creating a myriad of moiré patterns. The whole piece sits on a black granite base that appears to float on water.

PROJECT: *"Sapientia II"*

CLIENT: *Studio piece*

SIZE: *10 feet x 10 feet x 3 feet (3 meters x 3 meters x 1 meter)*

LOCATION: *Chatsworth, California*

A deep, polished, stainless steel frame filled with ripples, arcs, and slumped sheets of 1-inch-thick (2.5-cm-thick) etched glass, exploding into space. It reveals an underlying overlay of forms and lines.

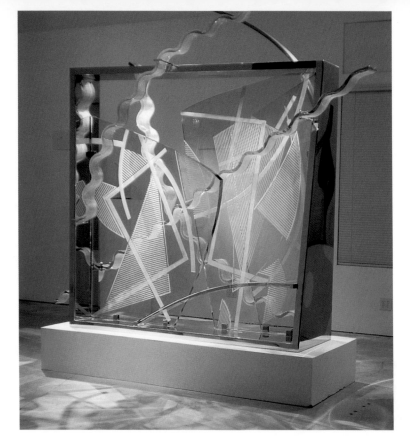

PROJECT: *Linear form series*

CLIENT: *Private residence*

SIZE: *4 feet x 4 feet x 12 feet (1.2 meters x 1.2 meters x 3.6 meters)*

LOCATION: *Lake Tahoe, Nevada*

Three sheets of 1-inch-thick (2.5-cm-thick) glass slumped into three different linear forms, etched with multiples of overlapping and intersecting lines and shapes. The piece is mounted into a three-level base, situated so as to be viewed from all sides as one descends the spiral staircase.

ARCHITECTURAL COMMISSIONS

American Airlines
JFK International Airport
New York, New York

Atlantic Richfield Company (ARCO)
Los Angeles, California

Carnation Company
Nestles Corporation
Glendale, California

Cumberland Center
Cobb County, Georgia
Cooper Cary and Associates, AIA

Hewlett-Packard
Mountain View, California

Hyatt on Collins
Melbourne, Australia

MCI
Atlanta, Georgia

Redken Cosmair Corporation
Clark, New Jersey

Royal Caribbean Cruise Lines
Copenhagen, Denmark

Supreme Court of Nevada
Carson City, Nevada

Yokohama Royal Park Hotel
Nikko, Japan

AFFILIATIONS

North Central College, Naperville, Illinois

California Lutheran University, Thousand Oaks, California (BA, fine arts)

University of California, Los Angeles, California (UCLA, MA, ceramics)

University of California, Los Angeles, California (UCLA, MFA, glass)

John Gilbert Luebtow

PROJECT: *Chapel window*

CLIENT: *St. Mary's Regional Health Center*

LOCATION: *Apple Valley, California*

ARCHITECT: *HBE Corporation, St. Louis, Missouri*

This window uses a woodcarved crucifix as the focal point.

PROJECT: *Resurrection window*

CLIENT: *St. Wendelin Catholic Church*

SIZE: *6 feet x 18 feet (1.8 meters x 5.5 meters)*

LOCATION: *Fostoria, Ohio*

ARCHITECT: *Dennis Mecham, Columbus, Ohio*

One of several leaded glass and sandblasted glass windows.

Maureen McGuire

924 East Bethany Home Road

Phoenix, Arizona 85014

602 277 0167 phone • 602 277 0203 fax

Maureen McGuire has walked a singular path throughout her life as an artist in stained glass. Childhood toys were supplemented or supplanted by those of her own making. Art training began early and few other occupations were ever seriously considered.

As an undergraduate student at Alfred University's New York State College of Ceramics during the "God is dead" era of the early 1960s, McGuire began creating designs in which He lived. Exercises in architecture became churches and chapels decorated by ceramic sculptures, woodcarvings in furniture designs, and graphic art. As the first design student allowed into what was until then the exclusive domain of the engineering school, McGuire began the first explorations in glass in a school now noted for its art glass program.

She continued her studies on scholarship at the Pope Pius XII Institute in Florence, Italy. There, she reinforced her connection to art history and symbolism and their importance in contemporary liturgical art. She worked in both stained glass and sculpture, receiving a Master's degree in 1964. The same year she accepted an offer to an apprentice position at the Glassart Studios in Scottsdale, Arizona. Honing her skills in all phases of the craft, she finally left Glassart's employ in 1968 to forge her own way as one of the United State's first independent stained glass designers.

Additional travel and studies with well-known German contemporary masters in architectural stained glass have strengthened Maureen's oeuvre. Following the demise of Glassart in 1987, McGuire established her own small studio to fill the gap left by Glassart and to satisfy her desire to better control some of her more innovative work. She continues to work with studios across the country principally, but not exclusively, in liturgically related commissions and still keeps active in sculpture and other forms of architectural art.

PROJECT: *Del Webb Corporate Center*

CLIENT: *Western Savings Company*

SIZE: *900 square feet (80 square meters)*

LOCATION: *Phoenix, Arizona*

ARCHITECT: *Cornoyer-Hedrick Associates, Pheonix, Arizona*

Leaded stained glass softens the light of the west facade and main entrance of a glass business mall structure.

PROJECT: *"The Conversion of St. Paul on the Road to Damascus"*

CLIENT: *St. Paul's Catholic Church*

SIZE: *500 square feet (44 square meters)*

LOCATION: *Phoenix, Arizona*

ARCHITECT: *Roberts-Jones Associates, Phoenix, Arizona*

Detail.

PROJECT: *Kitchen window*

CLIENT: *Bierny Residence*

SIZE: *9 feet x 9 feet (2.7 meters x 2.7 meters)*

LOCATION: *Tucson, Arizona*

FABRICATOR: *MMcGuire Design Associates, Phoenix, Arizona*

Leaded stained glass in a steel frame.

PROJECT: *Entry skylights*

CLIENT: *Lyon residence*

LOCATION: *Carefree, Arizona*

FABRICATOR: *Glassart Studio, Scottsdale, Arizona*

One of two clerestory windows to soften the east and west light in the living room.

ARCHITECTURAL COMMISSIONS

American Association of Retired Persons Corporate Headquarters
Washington, D.C.

Arizona State University Sun Devil Stadium
Papal Visit Mass
Tempe, Arizona

Church of the Holy Eucharist
Tabernacle, New Jersey

College View Seventh Day Adventist Church
Lincoln, Nebraska

Del E. Webb Corporate Center
Phoenix, Arizona

First Christian/Disciples of Christ Church
Las Vegas, Nevada

Lakeview United Methodist Church
Sun City, Arizona

Resurrection Mausoleum
St. Francis Cemetery
Phoenix, Arizona

St. Andrew Catholic Church
Cape Coral, Florida

St. Andrew the Apostle Catholic Church
Chandler, Arizona

St. Matthew's Baptist Church
Louisville, Kentucky

St. Paul's Catholic Church
Phoenix, Arizona

Woodlake Lutheran Church
Minneapolis, Minnesota

AFFILIATIONS

Interfaith Forum on Religion Art & Architecture, a division of the American Institute of Architects

A single tile, approximately 12 inches x 10 inches (31 centimeters x 25 centimeters) details the beautiful light quality that looks remarkably like water.

PROJECT: *"Waterwall"*

CLIENT: *Private Residence*

SIZE: *7 feet x 6 feet (2.1 meters x 1.8 meters)*

LOCATION: *Pawling, New York*

ARCHITECT: *Koupiek/Koustamitis*

The cast glass wall divides the spa from the indoor Olympic pool, allowing natural light in while obscuring the bathers.

(opposite page)

PROJECT: *"Check It Out!"*

CLIENT: *King County Library System*

SIZE: *7½ feet x 6½ feet (2.25 meters x 2 meters)*

LOCATION: *Bellevue, Washington*

ARCHITECT: *Zimmer Gunsul Frasca*

This interactive artwork, located at the main entry of a library, invites passersby to play with three different fresnel lenses that humorously distort their face.

4136 Meridian Avenue North

Seattle, Washington 98103

206 633 1901 phone • 206 632 1363 fax

Paul *Marioni and* Ann *Troutner*

Since 1977, Paul Marioni and Ann Troutner have completed more than fifty private and public architectural commissions using glass. Their primary concern is in making artwork that users can relate to, that addresses the architecture and the environment, and that is successful in its execution.

Much of Marioni and Troutner's work incorporates the medium of cast glass. They have helped to develop and expand this viable and practicable material, and they recommend the use of cast glass because of its multitudinous unique qualities. Cast glass is timeless and elegant and does not demand attention as an integral part of its environment.

Cast glass has the singular ability to capture, magnify, and manipulate the light, in any lighting situation: day or night, natural or artificial. With cast glass, imagery is perceived equally well from both sides, while both transmitting the light and obscuring the view. Cast glass can be used effectively as windows, walls, and entryways. Cast glass requires no maintenance and resists all but the most determined vandalism, which makes it an ideal medium for public settings. Its beauty makes it exceptional for private settings.

PROJECT: *"Shelter"*

CLIENT: *Washington State University Veterinary Hospital*

SIZE: *5 feet x 15 feet (1.5 meters x 4.5 meters)*

LOCATION: *Pullman, Washington*

ARCHITECT: *Deneff, Deeble, Barton Associates*

Two curving, 15-foot-long (4.5-meter-long) cast glass walls offer a private waiting area without obstructing this spacious lobby. The tall grass motif signifies food and shelter for the seventeen animals represented by their glass tracks flush-mounted into the terrazzo floor.

A single tile, 10 inches x 14 inches (25 centimeters x 36 centimeters), details the butterflies and seed pods. The grass blades bevel the light.

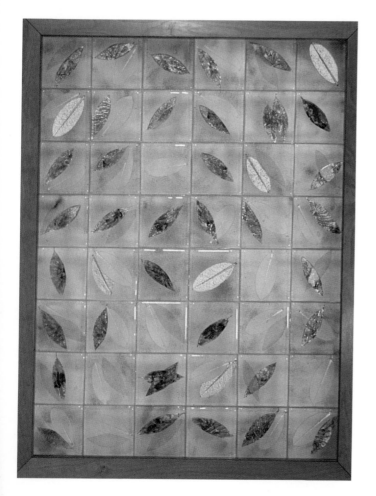

PROJECT: *"Golden Leaves"*

CLIENT: *Children's Hospital Chapel*

SIZE: *4 feet x 3 feet (1.2 meters x 1 meter)*

LOCATION: *Seattle, Washington*

The natural theme signifies serenity and rejuvenation for the human spirit of all faiths.

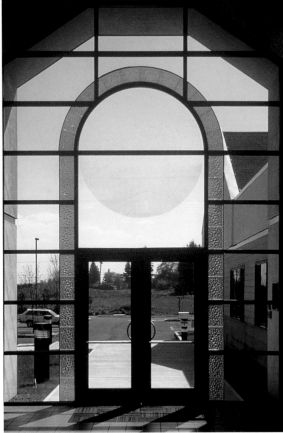

PROJECT: *"Elements"*

CLIENT: *Easthill Fire Station Headquarters*

SIZE: *18 feet x 12 feet (5.4 meters x 3.6 meters)*

LOCATION: *Kent, Washington*

ARCHITECT: *Christianson Architects*

(top left)
This exterior view shows a red-orange arch of dichroic glass, symbolizing fire. The sand-etched sphere adds a mystical quality to the entryway and mimics the thousands of cast lenses.

(top right)
This interior view of the same arch shows the dramatic change to a blue color, representing water.

ARCHITECTURAL COMMISSIONS

Children's Hospital
Seattle, Washington

Easthill Fire Station
Kent, Washington

Federal Parklands Project
Mt. Hood, Oregon

Greenlake Community Center
Seattle, Washington

King County Library System
Bellevue, Washington

Police/Fire Facility
Burbank, California

Port of Authority
Seattle, Washington

Rochester High School
Rochester, Washington

Univ. of Washington Medical Center
Seattle, Washington

Washington State University
Veterinary Hospital
Pullman, Washington

WIXT-TV
Syracuse, New York

Ziff Estate
Pawling, New York

AFFILIATIONS

Glass Art Society (member)

Canadian Glass Art Society (lifetime honorary membership)

PROJECT: *Cherokee Memorial Mausoleum*

CLIENT: *Cherokee Memorial Park*

SIZE: *1,000 square feet (90 square meters)*

LOCATION: *Lodi, California*

ARCHITECT: *J. C. Milne, Portland, Oregon*

The leaded art glass in this interfaith mausoleum chapel was designed to the client's desire to uplift and glorify the human life cycle and to have recognizable colorful forms. The limited palette intensifies the impact of the primary color in each wall. The art glass was chosen to block a view of the dark stairs beyond, and to tie the work to the clear glass. Pulling colors from neighboring windows into the curving vertical forms and the background grids maintains the unity of the space.

Jean Myers Architectural Glass

11 Willotta Drive

Suisun, California 94585

707 864 3906 phone • 707 864 3467 fax

Jean *Myers*

Jean Myers has chosen to work in stained glass for two very personal reasons. First of all, the medium allows her to create art that enhances and enriches the experiences of human life. Myers designs work that becomes part of settings where people live out the most important moments of their lives—in homes, places of worship, places where people work and study, and places where people recover physically and spiritually. Her objective is to bring the warmth and beauty she sees in the world to these everyday settings.

Secondly, Myers works in stained glass because, as an artist, she finds the medium offers her the most direct link between personal vision and completed creation. Those elements that fascinate her as an artist—color, light, shape, form, and the gifts of the natural world—come to life most vividly, most passionately, in stained glass.

The tools of Myers's trade are not new. Artists have worked in stained glass for centuries. And although the world is a far different place than that reflected in the windows at Sainte-Chapelle, for instance, she feels a kinship with the people who created those jewels of vision. They were after some spiritual triumph, some evidence that the soul and spirit of mankind could prevail. Myers shares that vision, and through her art seeks to express her own celebration of all that is brilliant, beautiful, and optimistic in the world.

Myers's work in architectural glass contributes a voice that soars and sings in color and light.

PROJECT: *Hallway and conference rooms*

CLIENT: *Fuqua Industries, Inc.*

LOCATION: *Atlanta, Georgia*

ARCHITECT: *HDR, Omaha, Nebraska*

The client wanted to match the high-image profile of the building, while expressing the chairman's classic modern taste, using Georgian earth tones. In the corridor linking the executive spaces, the stepped walls are finished with stained glass panels that impart a sense of light and color to the interior spaces. Stained glass panels surround clear and pure white glass, adding a calm, airy mood as well as elegance to an unusually shaped boardroom.

PROJECT: *Mercy Hospital Chapel*

CLIENT: *Mercy Hospital*

LOCATION: *Folsom, California*

Myers's challenge was to create an uplifting work in a room with no windows. It also had to be able to withstand potential earthquakes. Her creation is suspended and sways gently from the slight breeze of the air conditioner. The work creates dancing visions of light and brings life to a space that otherwise could have been oppressive.

PROJECT: *Sanctuary Windows*

CLIENT: *Christ the King Catholic Community Church*

LOCATION: *Las Vegas, Nevada*

The client made three requests: That the windows contain content associated with the Triduum, that the imagery be expressed in new symbolism, and that they contain the colors of their desert environment. Myers's windows were found to be a successful solution to the exploration of the mysteries of death and resurrection.

ARCHITECTURAL COMMISSIONS

Cherokee Memorial Park
Mausoleum
Lodi, California
Architect: J. C. Milne

Christ the King Catholic Community
Church
Las Vegas, Nevada
Architect: G. C. Wallace

First Christian Church
Portland, Oregon
Architect: J. Pecsok

Fuqua Industries, Inc.
Executive Offices
Atlanta, Georgia
Architect: HDR

Geist Christian Church
Indianapolis, Indiana
Architect: McGuire/Shock

Mercy Hospital
Folsom, California
Architect: Anderson, DeBartolo &
Pan

Our Savior's United Methodist
Church
Schaumberg, Illinois
Architect: Richard Kalb

St. Ignatius Catholic Church
Antioch, California
Architect: Mossbacker

St. Mark's in the Valley Episcopal
Church
Los Olivos, California
Architect: R. Barrett

Zionsville Presbyterian Church
Zionsville, Indiana
Architect: J. Pecsok

AFFILIATIONS

American Institute of Architects

Stained Glass Association of America

Marin Society of Artists

American Craft Council

PROJECT: *"Tower of the Ecliptic" observatory tower*

CLIENT: *Swansea Council*

SIZE: *16 ½ foot (5 meter) diameter*

LOCATION: *Swansea, Wales, U.K.*

ARCHITECT: *Robin Campbell*

The architect consulted with a glass artist, sculptor, and poet from the earliest stages of the design process. The glass provides a powerful, changing dynamic for the access tower. As one enters the tower, the glass ceiling encourages thoughts to turn to the cosmos, to greater worlds beyond our own, similar to the effect of a great cathedral.

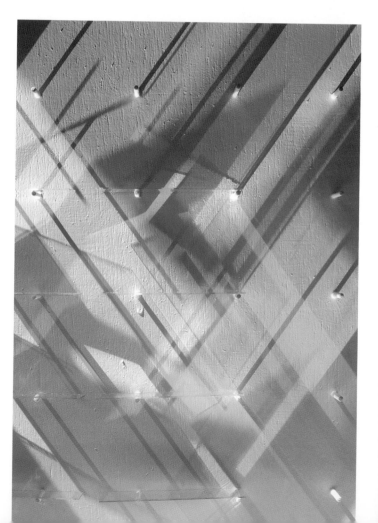

PROJECT: *Dichroic filter study*

CLIENT: *Booth and Company*

LOCATION: *Leeds, England, U.K.*

These are examples of a dichroic filter and lighting study executed for an upcoming installation. The work will be installed over four floors of a central atrium.

1 Greenfield Terrace

Sketty, Swansea SA2 9BS Wales, U.K.

44 179 229 6458 phone • 44 179 229 6458 fax

David *Pearl*

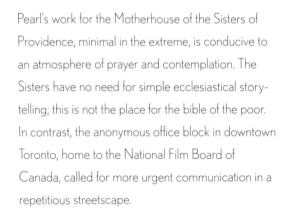

David Pearl's work resists the anonymity of the modern urban landscape. The artist intervenes to give voice to a building not merely as a decorator, but as a communicator. Pearl attempts to fuse the spirit of the user with the spirit of place. The eclectic nature of the artist's response defies ready formula and reflects the diversity of setting and client.

Pearl's work for the Motherhouse of the Sisters of Providence, minimal in the extreme, is conducive to an atmosphere of prayer and contemplation. The Sisters have no need for simple ecclesiastical story-telling; this is not the place for the bible of the poor. In contrast, the anonymous office block in downtown Toronto, home to the National Film Board of Canada, called for more urgent communication in a repetitious streetscape.

PROJECT: *"Inserted Landscape"*

CLIENT: *Canadian Clay and Glass Gallery*

LOCATION: *Waterloo, Ontario, Canada*

ARCHITECT: *Ian Gray*

A planted, part-glazed silo section sits in front of the gallery, its form reminiscent of both urban and rural architecture. The silo links the gallery to its immediate surroundings; the planted, water-filled concrete cylinder refers to the lake that once occupied the site. The layers of glass act as a lens on the past, each etched with details of historical maps that explore the changing nature of the surroundings.

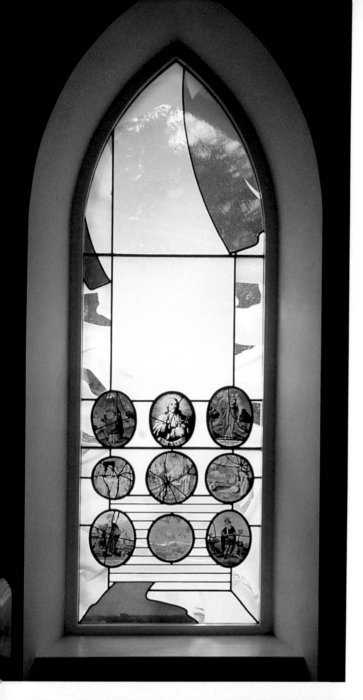

PROJECT: *Channel View Community Center*

CLIENT: *Channel View Community Center*

SIZE: *16½ feet x 16½ feet (5 meters x 5 meters)*

LOCATION: *Cardiff Bay, Wales, U.K.*

Glass panels depicting aerial surveys of the site from both conventional photographs and satellite images reflect the changing definition of community. The earliest aerial surveys in 1948 viewed the community in its own context from 1,000 feet (300 meters), whereas the modern viewer sees the past. The recent continuous satellite surveys put the community in a global context.

(top and bottom left)

PROJECT: *Missenden Abbey*

CLIENT: *Missenden Abbey*

LOCATION: *Buckinghamshire, England, U.K.*

Although most of the detailing such as the plaster work and stone floors were carefully restored, the glass was conceived as a dramatically modern counterpoint. The only element of color on the site, the acid-etched, south-facing French antique glass animates the interiors.

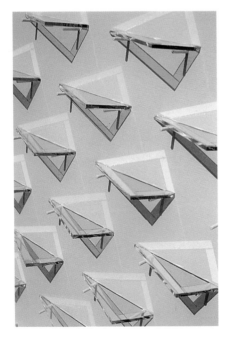

PROJECT: *Ove Arup installation*

CLIENT: *Ove Arup Engineers*

LOCATION: *Cardiff, Wales, U.K.*

Detail of their twenty-fifth anniversary commission.

PROJECT: *Grand Theater*

CLIENT: *Grand Theater*

SIZE: *1,100 square feet (100 square meters)*

LOCATION: *Swansea, Wales, U.K.*

The design utilizes custom-produced Lamberts opal glass to create a colored atmosphere. The proportions and forms echo the geometry of the architecture.

ARCHITECTURAL COMMISSIONS

Booth and Company
Leeds, England, U.K.

Canadian Clay and Glass Gallery
Waterloo, Ontario, Canada

Channel View Community Center
Cardiff Bay, Wales, U.K.

Grand Theater
Swansea, Wales, U.K.

Missenden Abbey
Buckinghamshire, England, U.K.

Ove Arup Engineers
Cardiff, Wales, U.K.

"Tower of the Ecliptic"
Swansea, Wales, U.K.

PROJECT: *One of seven windows in the Festival Hall of The Wiesbaden City Hall, 1989*

CLIENT: *The City of Wiesbaden*

SIZE: *4 feet x 6¼ feet (1.2 meters x 1.9 meters)*

LOCATION: *Wiesbaden, Germany*

ARCHITECT: *Städt. Hochbauamt Wiesbaden*

(opposite page)

PROJECT: *Police Academy, Window in the lobby, 1983*

CLIENT: *The State of Nordrhein-Westfalen*

SIZE: *33 feet x 19 feet (10 meters x 5.7 meters)*

LOCATION: *Münster-Hiltrup, Germany*

ARCHITECT: *Staatschochbauamt Münster, Germany*

Floatglass, handblown, leaded, opalescent flashed glass.

Heinemann-Musoge-Weg 8

59494 Soest, Germany

49 2921 73533 phone • 49 2921 73731 fax

Jochem *Poensgen*

Walter Benjamin introduced the architectural concept of "reception through use" sixty years ago in his book, *The Work of Art in the Age of Reproduction.* Jochem Poensgen feels strongly that stained glass artists also should realize and accept "civil inattention" as a widespread and a rather appropriate attitude toward architecture and architectural art.

The work of glass artists, alone and through collaboration with architects, would benefit if the artist gave up demanding constant attention for his work. This is no easy task for devoted artists. Poensgen freely admits that it took him quite some time to accept, and even interpret in a positive light, the notion of "civil inattention" as a reaction to many of his windows.

Today Poensgen finds it easy to embrace this attitude and adapt his work accordingly when he approves of the architecture his work is meant to interpret. This is precisely the case whenever the architecture itself—through an intelligent and dignified simplicity and serenity—simply aims at being casually noticed through the course of an everyday familiarity.

For years glass artists have been obsessed with finding the freedom and independence that is the prerequisite of glass work. Glass artists have had to abandon burdensome traditions and find new, hitherto unknown techniques. But Poensgen believes his contemporaries should by now have reached a degree of self-confidence to concentrate on their task and to do a good job—no more, no less. To Poensgen that simply means doing what's appropriate in a relaxed way.

PROJECT: *"Concept for a Glass Tower," Autonomous object, 1996*

CLIENT: *Private collection*

SIZE: *1¼ feet x 1¼ feet x 4 feet (40 centimeters x 40 centimeters x 1.2 meters)*

LOCATION: *Germany*

Floatglass (sandblasted), reeded glass, stainless steel and wooden base.

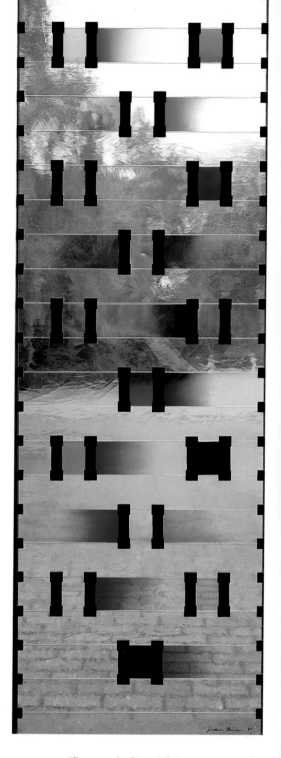

PROJECT: *"Between the Lines 1," Autonomous panel*

CLIENT: *Private collection*

SIZE: *2 feet x 6 feet (60 centimeters x 1.8 meters)*

LOCATION: *Kleve, Germany*

Handblown, acid-etched antique glass. The individual pieces are held together by lead "corners."

PROJECT: *Room Divider in Two Layers*
Interior Screen, 1990

CLIENT: *Museum für Kunsthandwerk, Germany*

SIZE: *7 feet x 1 inch x 7 feet (2.1 meters x 3
centimeters x 2.1 meters)*

LOCATION: *Frankfurt/Main, Germany*

*In two layers: Floatglass, handblown antique and opales-
cent glass, bevels, lead H-pieces (incomplete leading).*

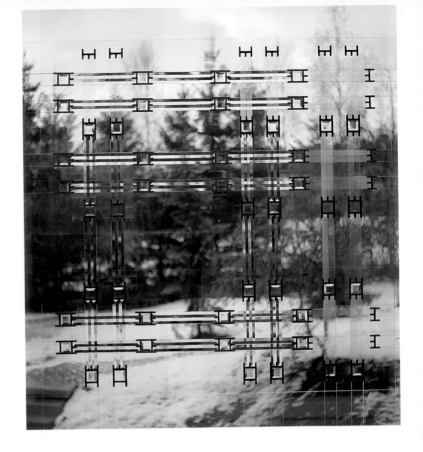

PROJECT: *One of four window areas in St. Andreas
Catholic Church, 1993–1998*

CLIENT: *Parish of St. Andreas*

LOCATION: *Essen-Rüttenscheid, Germany*

ARCHITECT: *Rudolf Schwarz (1897–1961)*

Section of window in St. Andreas Catholic Church

ARCHITECTURAL COMMISSIONS

Cemetery Ornäskyrkogården
Luleå, Sweden

City Hall
Wiesbaden, Germany

Courthouse
Büdingen, Germany

Dresdner Bank AG
Hamburg, Germany

Fulda Cathedral, St. Boniface Vault
Germany

Hospital
Davos-Wolfgang, Switzerland

Lutheran Church Maria-zur-Höhe
Soest, Germany

Police Academy
Münster-Hiltrup, Germany

St. Andreas Catholic Church
Essen-Rüttenscheid, Germany

Textile Store Klingenthal
Paderborn, Germany

AFFILIATIONS

Augustinermuseum
Freiburg, Germany

Corning Museum of Glass
Corning, New York

Hess. Landesmuseum
Darmstadt, Germany

Museum für Kunsthandwerk
Frankfurt a. M., Germany

Städt. Kunstmuseum
Düsseldorf, Germany

Victoria & Albert Museum
London, England

Since 1991: Visiting Professor at
Swansea Institute, Faculty of Art &
Design
Architectural Glass Department,
Swansea, England

PROJECT: *Elson residence*

LOCATION: *New York, New York*

A screen of leaded, blown glass with bevels and a Venetian-blown rondel was designed for a sophisticated Manhattan penthouse as part of the client's art collection. The minimal, linear vocabulary of the project represents a departure from the way Quagliata typically designs pieces for private spaces. Executed by Dorothy Lenehan.

(opposite page)

PROJECT: *Private residence*

LOCATION: *Mexico City, Mexico*

Leaded, blown glass with custom-blown rondels and bevels.

25125 Santa Clara Street, #155

Hayward, California 94544

Contact: Fran Bennett

510 888 2415 phone • 510 537 1412 fax

Narcissus *Quagliata*

Narcissus Quagliata's understanding of architecture and knowledge of glass come together in his ability to integrate glass into each environment with unique solutions that enhance the integrity of a building's overall design. The works shown here represent four such solutions for installations with distinctly different tastes, cultures, and environments. Quagliata is at home in the U.S., Mexico, and Europe.

Quagliata began his career in stained glass in the early 1970s and soon transformed conventional techniques to suit his images and aesthetic perception. He pushed the medium to its limits, achieving an unparalleled level of intricacy and finesse.

Quagliata's recent works represent a complete merging of glass and painting in a process that utilizes the latest technical innovations. The imagery is freely created on a glass surface, then fired in a kiln. As he works, he is not only designing a piece but also inventing the medium. His involvement with glass at both technical and creative levels has resulted in his being sponsored by industrial companies, currently Bullseye Glass, to develop an aesthetic language for their new fusible glass.

Glass in architecture can affect light in such a way as to improve the quality of life and create a sense of well-being. Quagliata sees himself as entrusted with bringing light and joy into a space, whether it be public or private. He works with glass because it reveals light, and he is interested in light because, he says, it is existence itself.

PROJECT: *Yerba Buena Parking Facility*

LOCATION: *San Francisco, California*

Sandblasted, laminated, and fused glass lit with neon become railings of light in this elegant solution to the design of a parking garage.

PROJECT: *"Gateway into Night"*

SIZE: *12 feet x 30 feet (3.7 meters x 9 meters); 108 panels, each 19 inches x 19 inches (48 centimeters x 48 centimeters) with life-size human silhouette cast in clear glass*

The first monumental work ever to employ the technique of light painting, "Gateway into Night" illustrates that glass is not only a decorative medium, but a powerful vehicle for the expression of ideas about the human psyche and existence. Created for museum exhibition, this work of light painting and fused glass is held together by a high-tech frame system that allows for easy travel.

ARCHITECTURAL COMMISSIONS

Alachua County Library
Gainesville, Florida

Alice Art Center
Oakland, California

Charles Schwab Building Lobby
San Francisco, California

Library of the Department of
Engineering
National University of Mexico
Mexico City, Mexico

Pacific Bell Building Lobby
Oakland, California

Private residences in the U.S., Italy,
and Mexico

AFFILIATIONS

Bullseye Glass Company, Portland, Oregon
Dorothy Lenehan Glass Design, Emeryville, California
Studio of Miriam Di Fiore, Milan, Italy
Studio Vitrum, Mexico City, Mexico

PROJECT: *"Twelve Words for Ice," cast glass entry*

CLIENT: *Recreational Equipment Inc. (REI)*

SIZE: *each panel, 1 foot x 1¼ feet (30 centimeters x 40 centimeters)*

LOCATION: *Seattle, Washington*

View from inside of front entry with twelve cast glass panels. Detail (opposite page) shows the texture of the cast glass.

Detail showing texture of kiln-cast glass.

PROJECT: *Free-standing glass screen*

CLIENT: *Parsons, Fernandez, and Casteleiro*

SIZE: *6 feet x 12 feet (1.8 meters x 3.6 meters)*

LOCATION: *New York, New York*

This piece is made of kiln-cast glass and is meant for a building lobby.

Contemporary Art Glass

P.O. Box 31422

Seattle, Washington 98103

206 527 5022 phone • 206 524 9226 fax

www.mayaglass.com website

Maya *Radoczy*

Maya Radoczy applies original glass techniques to create site-specific corporate, public, and residential projects, as well as sculptural concepts. She is known for forming unusual surfaces in glass and molded relief images with cast, fused, hand-blown, and leaded glass techniques. She works with architects, designers, and art consultants to develop unique solutions for the use of art glass in architecture. She has created numerous large-scale commissions, including a free-standing conference room, sculptural screens for corporate lobbies, murals, and mobiles for atrium spaces. Exhibiting her work nationally and internationally, she has won awards and has been featured in many publications and collections.

Demonstrating balance and openness in her work, she allows the architectural space to be a catalyst for the art glass. In a recent commission for the new REI building in Seattle, the client wanted to make use of raw materials and natural light to represent the wilderness and mountain-climbing. Radoczy employed translucent cast glass to connect the outside light with the beautifully designed inner architectural spaces. The sculptured glass panels are an abstract interpretation of various glacial surfaces and geological formations, and the surface engages the viewer and gently transmits light.

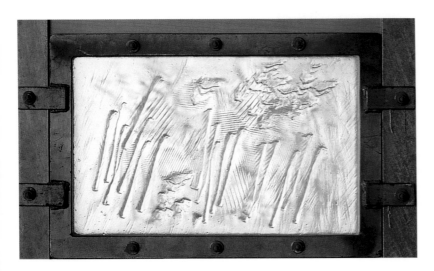

Detail of cast-glass for REI entry (one of twelve different images).

PROJECT: *"Photon Interspace"*

CLIENT: *Marin General Hospital*

SIZE: *7 feet x 14 feet (2.1 meters x 4.2 meters)*

LOCATION: *San Rafael, California*

This piece was for a hospital atrium space and consists of thousands of hand-pulled glass threads fused together with metal framing. The threads represent the scatter patterns of sub-atomic particle collisions.

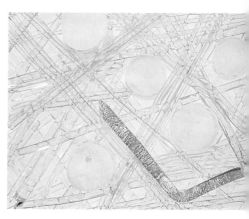

Detail

PROJECT: *"Gaia Reflections"*

CLIENT: *Linpro Corporation*

SIZE: *100 square feet (9 square meters)*

LOCATION: *Three Christina Center, Wilmington, Delaware*

This free-standing screen for the building entry was created with hand-blown, fused, and leaded glass. The bold design was intended to be seen at night by passing cars. It also features details that can be seen at close range by people using the lobby.

PROJECT: *"Myth and Magic in the City"*

CLIENT: *Lynnwood Library*

SIZE: *5 feet x 12 feet (1.5 meters x 3.6 meters)*

LOCATION: *Lynnwood, Washington*

This hand-blown and leaded glass mural was created for the children's section of a library. It uses many fused glass elements, and thematically refers to stories, myths, astronomical events: subjects that a child might read about in the library.

Detail.

ARCHITECTURAL COMMISSIONS

Colville Elementary School
Colville, Washington

Bogle & Gates Law Offices
Seattle, Washington

Intrex Inc.
New York, New York

Linpro Corporation
Wilmington, Delaware

Lynwood Library
Lynwood, Washington

Marin General Hospital
San Rafael, California

Recreational Equipment Inc.
Seattle, Washington

Trump Plaza
New York, New York

University Hospital
Seattle, Washington

U.S. Bank
Seattle, Washington

AFFILIATIONS

Glass Art Society (member)
Pratt Fine Arts Center, Seattle, Washington
Cornish Institute School of Design, Seattle, Washington
Pilchuck School, Stanwood, Washington
New England School of Art and Design, Boston, Massachusetts

(top)

PROJECT:	*Apartment*
CLIENT:	*Mr. and Mrs. F. Cielak*
SIZE:	*130 square feet (12 square meters)*
LOCATION:	*Mexico City, Mexico*
ARCHITECT:	*Agraz and Gitlin*

This screen features movable windows for the occasional integration of the studio with the living room. The composition is a continuation of the wood molding design, which converts into glass strips with brilliant and opaque contrasts.

(left)

PROJECT:	*Director's Bank offices*
SIZE:	*19 feet x 9 feet (5.7 meters x 2.7 meters)*
LOCATION:	*Mexico City, Mexico*
ARCHITECT:	*Megarquitectos, S.A.*

In this screen for the bank director's main entrance, the theme is an abstraction of a bank's vault and money. The bank's corporate colors are used in the design.

(opposite page)

PROJECT:	*Private residence*
CLIENT:	*Mr. and Mrs. D. Cherem*
SIZE:	*6 feet x 4½ feet (1.8 meters x 1.5 meters)*
LOCATION:	*Estado de Mexico, Mexico*
ARCHITECT:	*Daniel Cherem*

A zigzag screen that shows different designs when moved, allowing the observer to enjoy and participate in this kinetic piece.

Calle Uno No. 4 Depto. 1

Col. San Pedro de los Pinos

03800 Mexico, D.F., Mexico

52 5 272 8674 phone • 52 5 272 8674 fax

José Antonio *Rage Mafud*

José Antonio Rage Mafud's work in stained glass is best understood from an architectural point of view, where his pieces bring light and space face-to-face in an intimate rite to create specific atmospheres. His compositions are based on geometric abstractions, where chaos and order are contained within the structures. Rage Mafud's fragile thematic amalgams often give birth to new motifs, ones in which rhythmic elements order the play of light in a kinetic space.

In his work, the control of a viewpoint, the filtering of an image, and the framing of perspectives are excuses to mold the light. In his own special way he converts the stained glass into a zone where light changes its vestments; where the interior and exterior meet and become one. Rage Mafud's professional perception as an architect allows him to read and understand each space's specific possibilities and limitations, always striving to take advantage of both. This effort makes the development of each of his projects unique and unable to be duplicated.

Whether it be in either of the techniques he uses, leaded or laminated—Rage Mafud's specialty—he reconciles the elements of architecture, functionality, and construction at the point where premise and concept become one.

In Rage Mafud's commissions it is easy to understand how stained glass—as well as architecture— is a crucible where the alchemist is transformed to the same degree as is the matter itself, where light is creativity.

PROJECT: *ING Insurance offices*

CLIENT: *ING Insurance*

SIZE: *810 square feet (75 square meters)*

LOCATION: *Mexico City, Mexico*

ARCHITECT: *Megarquitectos, S.A.*

The laminated glass screen that divides the reception area from the working area is searching for visual but not aural communication. The design of both pieces is complementary.

PROJECT: *Restaurant*

CLIENT: *El Tizoncito*

SIZE: *11 ½ feet x 11 feet (3.5 meters x 3.2 meters)*

LOCATION: *Mexico City, Mexico*

ARCHITECTS: *Jorge Alcocer y José Antonio Rage*

The perforated walls and interrupted railings give emphasis to the visual ends and spatial continuity in an evident play of light and shadow.

PROJECT: *Apartment*

CLIENT: *Mr. and Mrs. Fermon*

SIZE: *2 1/4 feet x 2 1/2 feet (.7 meter x .8 meter)*

LOCATION: *Mexico City, Mexico*

ARCHITECT: *Jorge Vera Ferrer*

The use of light colors and bevels increased the luminosity of this space. The design uses a rich variety of sparkling, opaque, and textured glass and accents of color with fused pieces.

PROJECT: *Apartment building*

CLIENT: *Lic. Gerardo Martínez C.*

SIZE: *6 feet x 6 feet (1.8 meters x 1.8 meters)*

LOCATION: *Mexico City, Mexico*

ARCHITECTS: *Jorge Tena García y Jorge Tena Urbina*

Because of its coloring and the use of opalescent glass, this window has a strong presence both inside and outside. The geometric form is interrupted at a specific point to provide a relationship with the exterior scenery.

ARCHITECTURAL COMMISSIONS

Autonomous Metropolitan
University
Mexico City, Mexico

Iberoamerican University
Mexico City, Mexico

ING Insurance
Mexico City, Mexico

Mexican Postal Service
Mexico City, Mexico

President's Staff
Mexico City, Mexico

Rothschild Bank
Mexico City, Mexico

Secretariat of Public Education
Mexico City, Mexico

ING Bank
Mexico City, Mexico

Mexican Senate
Mexico City, Mexico

AFFILIATIONS

Asociación de Artistas del Vidrio, A.C. (AAV)/The Mexican Glass Art Association

Colegio de Arquitectos de la Ciudad de México (CAM-SAM)/The Mexico City Architects Guild

PROJECT: *St. Bernard Church, 1995*

LOCATION: *Hamburg, Germany*

Execution by Oidtmann Studio.

PROJECT: *Wiesbaden Town Hall, 1989*

CLIENT: *City of Wiesbaden*

LOCATION: *Wiesbaden, Germany*

Windows on a staircase. Execution by Derix, Taunusstein.

Theodor-Seipp-Strasse 118

52477 Alsdorf-Ofden, Germany

49 2404 1243 phone • 49 2404 24010 fax

Ludwig *Schaffrath*

Ludwig Schaffrath's career began in 1947 when he accepted a faculty position as a lecturer on free-hand drawing in the architecture department at the Rheinisch-Westfälische Technische Hoschule. In addition to lecturing at schools and universities in various countries including Japan, Australia, and the United Kingdom, in 1985 he became a professor at Staatliche Akademie der Bildenden Künste in Stuttgart, Germany.

PROJECT: *Private residence, 1982*
LOCATION: *Aachen-Rott, Germany*

Execution by Oidtmann Studio.

PROJECT: *Haus der kirchlichen Dienste*

LOCATION: *Friedrichshafen, Germany*

Glass wall.

PROJECT: *St. Leonhard Church, 199.*

LOCATION: *Frankfurt, Germany*

Execution by Oidtmann Studio.

PROJECT: *St. Lioba College, 1993*

LOCATION: *Bad Nauheim, Germany*

Execution by Oidtmann Studio.

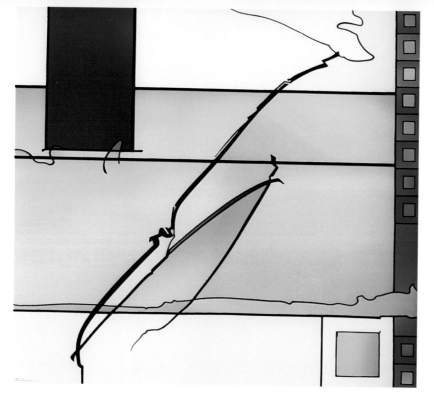

PROJECT: *Gallery house window*

CLIENT: *K. Kajiwara*

SIZE: *4¹/₄ feet x 5 feet (1.3 meters x 1.5 meters)*

LOCATION: *Hita-City, Oita, Japan*

Window for the Kajiwara gallery house. Execution by Derix, Taunusstein.

(opposite page)

PROJECT: *Church window*

CLIENT: *Paulus Community*

SIZE: *9¹/₂ feet x 4¹/₂ feet (2.9 meters x 1.4 meters)*

LOCATION: *Rauenberg, Germany*

ATCHITECT: *Veit Ruser, Karlsruhe*

Window in the religious service hall. Execution by Derix, Taunusstein.

PROJECT: *Window for the election chapel, Frankfurt Cathedral*

CLIENT: *Bischöfliches Ordinariat, Limburg*

SIZE: *8¹/₄ feet x 4¹/₂ feet (2.5 meters x 1.4 meters)*

LOCATION: *Frankfurt, Germany*

A grave divides a carpet of light from a carpet of darkness. A part of humanity lives in light and comfort but the majority live in suppressed darkness. At bottom left there is a reconciliation display. (The small chapel was the election place of kings and emperors of the Holy Roman Empire of the German Nation.) Execution by Derix, Taunusstein.

Rothkehlchenweg 7

63225 Langen, Germany

49 6103 71468 phone • 49 6103 71468 fax

Johannes *Schreiter*

Johannes Schreiter, born in 1930 in Annaberg-Buchholz/Erzgebirge, Germany, studied at the Westphalia Art School Münster, University of Mainz, and the Academy of Fine Arts, Berlin. In 1958 he won a scholarship to the Friedrich-Ebert-Stiftung, Bonn, where he invented his fire collage. From 1960 to 1963, he was director of the department *Fläche* in the School of Art in Bremen; in 1963 he moved to the Academy of Fine Arts, Frankfurt, where he was professor, head of the department of painting and graphics, and, from 1971 to 1974, president.

Since 1975, Johannes Schreiter has increasingly concerned himself with architectural art, primarily in the form of stained glass. He is best known outside of Germany for his work in window design, but his immense output in the field of graphics is also impressive.

Examples of his graphic work and window designs are collected in more than sixty international galleries and museums. Since 1960, he has completed many stained glass window commissions for churches and secular buildings. Awards include a gold medal in the Second International Biennale in Salzburg, 1960, an award at the exhibition "Contemporary European Graphic Art" in Salzburg 1974, and the Philip Morris prize for painting in 1977. In 1974 he received the BVK (the Cross of Merit of West Germany) and in 1984 the Medal of Honour at the second exhibition "Kleine Grafische Formen" in Lodz, Poland. He has lectured in Great Britain, the U.S., Canada, New Zealand, and Australia, with exhibitions in Europe, the U.S., Africa, Japan, New Zealand, Alaska, Brazil, India, and Russia.

PROJECT: *Window for St. Franziskus Church*

CLIENT: *Church Community*

SIZE: *20½ feet x 10 feet (6.2 meters x 3 meters)*

LOCATION: *Bad Kreuznach, Germany*

ARCHITECT: *Thomas Stahlheber*

Window dedicated to Klaus Eickhoff. Execution by Derix, Taunusstein.

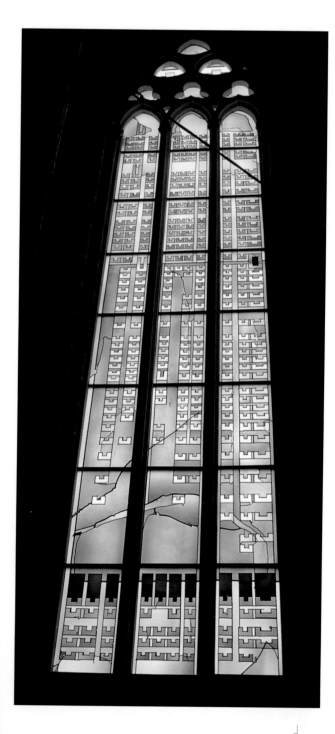

PROJECT: *Window for the Marktkirche*

CLIENT: *Church Community*

SIZE: *28¼ feet x 6¼ feet (8.6 meters x 1.9 meters)*

LOCATION: *Goslar, Germany*

Choir window located on the northeast side of the church. Execution by Derix, Taunusstein.

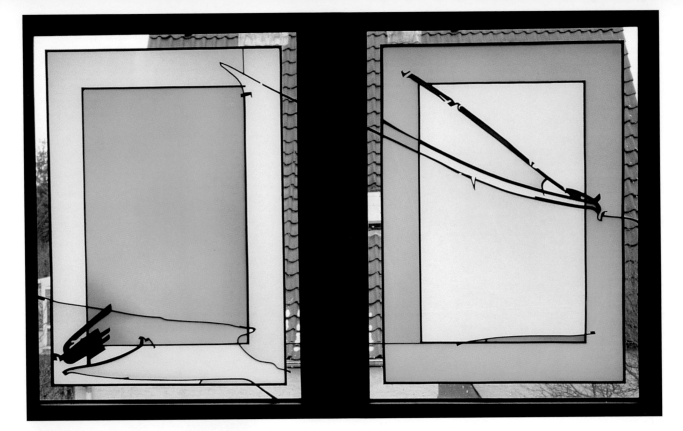

PROJECT: *Studio windows*

CLIENT: *Prof. Dr. J. Meyer*

SIZE: *3 ¼ feet x 2 ¾ feet (1 meter x .8 meter) each*

LOCATION: *Bremerhaven, Germany*

What is visible through the imitation passepartouts is in a meditative colorfield context with a lead sketch: introduction for tension and release (G. Sehring). Execution by Derix, Taunusstein.

ARCHITECTURAL COMMISSIONS

Airport Chapel
Frankfurt, Germany

Christus Church
St. Ingert, Germany

Evangelical Church of Hessen and Nassau
Darmstadt, Germany

Foreign Office
Bonn, Germany

Frankfurt Cathedral
Frankfurt, Germany

Grunewald Church
Berlin, Germany

Kajiwara Gallery
Hita-City, Japan

Reconciliation Church
Plauen, Germany

St. Franziskus Church
Bad Kreuznach, Germany

AFFILIATIONS

Deutscher Künstlerbund

Westdeutscher Künstlerbund

Neue Darmstädter Sezession

PROJECT: *Window for the Chancellery Office Building*

CLIENT: *Evangelical Church of Hessen and Nassau*

SIZE: *10 feet x 4 feet (3 meters x 1.2 meters)*

LOCATION: *Darmstadt, Germany*

Staircase windows. Execution by Derix, Taunusstein.

PROJECT: *Library window*

CLIENT: *Utah Arts Council*

SIZE: *12 ½ feet x 27 ½ feet (3.8 meters x 8.3 meters)*

LOCATION: *Salt Lake City, Utah*

ARCHITECT: *Astle Ericson Associates, Salt Lake City*

A palette of filmy white glass and contrasting textures of clear, colorless glass add interest to the spatial flow between this reading area and the atrium beyond.

PROJECT: *Ceiling stained glass,
St. Michael Chapel*

CLIENT: *St. Michael Health Care Center*

SIZE: *20 feet x 22 feet (6 meters x 6.5 meters)*

LOCATION: *Texarkana, Texas*

ARCHITECT: *Watkins Carter Hamilton Architects, Houston, Texas*

The ceiling of this windowless chapel is backlit with fluorescent lighting. The stained glass panels within its ceiling grid are individually framed beneath a mirror that has been partially etched with a complementary design. Etched areas allow light through, while the silvered areas reflect subtle imagery downward. The overall interior view of the chapel is highlighted here.

Architectural Stained Glass, Inc.

P.O. Box 9092

Dallas, Texas 75209

214 352 5050 phone • 214 827 5000 fax

Jeff G. Smith

The unique glass art of Jeff G. Smith reflects his introduction to stained glass in the early 1970s as part of Paul A. Dufour's groundbreaking Stained Glass Program at Louisiana State University's Fine Arts Department. He later studied with two of the great post-war German glass designers, Ludwig Schaffrath and Johannes Schreiter. Upon graduation in 1977, Smith established Architectural Stained Glass, Inc. in Dallas, Texas.

Two complementary subdivisions become evident when reviewing Smith's work. Autonomous stained glass is an outgrowth of his earliest academic efforts. These critically acclaimed free-hanging panels are conceptually similar to easel painting and continue to provide a manageable crucible within which new glass ideas are explored and perfected.

Autonomous stained glass is a dream world counterpart to the "real" world of his architectural stained glass. Just as dreams sometimes overlap our waking moments, Smith's autonomous ideas often unexpectedly turn up in his architectural stained glass.

Smith was first attracted to architectural uses of stained glass by the possibility of a deeper appreciation of this elusive medium as a fully three-dimensional experience. Smith's architectural work allows glass's transparency to subtly enhance views while using its contrasting obscurity for screening. His installations anticipate and take advantage of sunlight throughout daily and seasonal cycles yet also have a rich nighttime presence. Painstaking project analysis combined with a collaborative design process prepare Smith for the sensitive integration of stained glass into the overall architectural fabric as a dynamically appropriate element.

The common thread running throughout Smith's work is a reverence for the transcendent transparency of glass. By not overemphasizing the two-dimensional picture plane of the window itself, Smith is able to concentrate on the incredible, multidimensional possibilities for filtering, reflecting, refracting, and projecting light through and beyond windows.

PROJECT:	*"The Five Books of Moses"*
CLIENT:	*Washington Hebrew Congregation*
SIZE:	*Five windows, each 11 feet x 8 feet (3.2 meters x 2.3 meters)*
LOCATION:	*Washington, D.C.*
ART CONSULTANT:	*Elizabeth Michaels Associates*

The Five Books of Moses (Genesis, Exodus, Leviticus, Numbers, and Deuteronomy) greet visitors to this synagogue as seen in this exterior view at dusk. Numerous aspects of each book are represented through an abstract narrative design. The diverse palette of glass provides a dynamic, ever-changing experience, whether the windows are viewed from the outside or from the lobby inside. The rich imagery of each of the Books of Moses are symbolized through abstract, narrative symbolism in each of the windows.

PROJECT:	*Jacuzzi windows*
CLIENT:	*Ed H. Smith residence*
SIZE:	*19 square feet (1.7 square meters)*
LOCATION:	*Pine Bluff, Arkansas*

The partially etched and backlit mirror installed behind the stained glass ensures both total privacy and a dynamic variety of experience in this window during day or night. Dichroic accents contribute a shifting sparkle of color in this daylight view with interior lighting.

PROJECT: *"Hope Chapel"*

CLIENT: *Childrens and Presbyterian Healthcare Center*

SIZE: *855 square feet (77 square meters)*

LOCATION: *Plano, Texas*

ARCHITECTS: *Hermanovski Lauck Design and HKS Architects, Dallas, Texas*

Privacy and solitude within this prismatic interdenominational chapel are threatened by its location at the intersection of two building wings. A receding drapery-like night sky of etched glass stars are utilized to both screen the building wings and to provide counterpoint to the higher spiritual plane symbolized at the center.

PROJECT: *Conference room window*

CLIENT: *AARP*

SIZE: *6 feet x 4 feet (1.8 meters x 1.2 meters)*

LOCATION: *Washington, D.C.*

This window separates a brightly illuminated conference room from a dimly lit corridor. In addition to mouth-blown glass, accents of dichroic glass change apparent color as one moves along the corridor.

ARCHITECTURAL COMMISSIONS

American Federal Bank Lobby
Dallas, Texas

Ellis II Maximum Security Prison Chapel
Huntsville, Texas

Life Center Stairwell
San Francisco, California

Palace Rotunda Suspended Sculpture
Riyadh, Saudi Arabia

Presbyterian Hospital Chapel
Plano, Texas

Sandcastle Retreat
Clearwater, Florida

Sheraton Grand Hotel Porte Cochere
Houston, Texas

St. Alcuin Montessori School Gymnasium and Hallways
Dallas, Texas

St. Mary Immaculate Church Sanctuary
Plainfield, Illinois

St. Michael Healthcare Center Chapel Ceiling
Texarkana, Texas

Worthen National Bank Entry Foyer
Pine Bluff, Arkansas

Wilcox Memorial Hospital Meditation Chapel
Lihue, Kauai, Hawaii

AFFILIATIONS

Stained Glass Association of America

Glass Art Society

American Craft Council

Interfaith Forum on Religion Art and Architecture

Construction Specifiers Institute

PROJECT: *"Sentinels"*

CLIENT: *R. B. Long Federal Courthouse*

SIZE: *12½ feet x 17 feet (3.8 meters x 5 meters)*

LOCATION: *Baton Rouge, Louisiana*

All three installations for this National GSA Percent for the Arts Project share the same design vocabulary and are inspired by the architecture. They are built entirely of handblown glass with large prisms, hand-beveled from thick plate glass. While most of the window is opaque, there are windows within the window, irregular openings that allow a vista through to the city beyond.

(opposite page)

PROJECT: *Kitchen window*

CLIENT: *Artist's home*

SIZE: *6 feet x 4 feet (1.8 meters x 1.2 meters)*

LOCATION: *Sausalito, California*

Leaded glass with beveled glass jewels. This window is in the artist's home. It allows beautiful natural light to enter the room while at the same time filtering out an undesirable view.

Arthur Stern Studios
1075 Jackson Street
Benicia, California 94510
707 745 8480 phone • 707 745 8480 fax

Arthur *Stern*

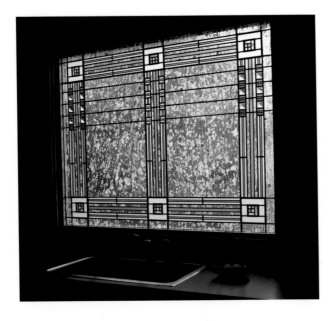

Arthur Stern comes out of an American glass tradition, drawing inspiration from Frank Lloyd Wright and the Prairie School. He has used Wright's geometric glass detailing as a departure point for his own designs. Also a student of the work of German postwar glass designers like Schreiter, Schaffrath, and Poensgen, the artist has combined these influences into a unique design sensibility strongly inspired by architecture. He considers himself a designer first and an artist second, and creates each installation with sensitivity to its specific environment.

The artist also works in other media, including works on paper, mixed-media paintings, and sculpture, and often incorporates glass into these autonomous works of art as well. Working within a family of design or variations on a theme, Stern has used certain geometric symbols and repeating motifs over the years. Much like a musician, he uses this language as a basis for improvisation. All the work shares a similar evolving design vocabulary.

Stern studied architecture at the University of Illinois and Environmental Design at the California College of Arts and Crafts. Since 1976, he has owned and operated Arthur Stern Studios, now located in Benicia, California. The studio has installations throughout the United States as well as in Japan, creating unique and site-specific works of art for residential, commercial, and public building projects. Stern has been widely published and has won numerous awards, including several from the American Institute of Architects.

PROJECT: "Torchere"

CLIENT: R. B. Long Federal Courthouse

SIZE: 8 feet x 5 feet x 6 inches (3 meters x 1.5 meters x 15.2 centimeters)

LOCATION: Baton Rouge, Louisiana

The lobby sculpture is an 8-foot-tall (2.4-meter-tall) bas-relief of cherry wood and leaded glass, lit only with reflected ambient light. The leaded glass incorporates gold and bronze handblown mirrors as part of the palette of materials, reflecting light from the main entrance. The shapes of the sculpture are inspired by exterior columns flanking the entrance. The lobby's wainscot and doors are cherry wood, another site-specific feature of the installation.

PROJECT: "Zig Zag Frozen Music"

SIZE: 6 feet x 2³/₄ feet x 2 feet (1.8 meters x .8 meter x .6 meter)

This double-glazed cantilevered sculpture offers a changing vista through the two leaded glass panels. The free-standing sculptural piece consists of two identical panels mounted back-to-back. The empty space between them creates an intriguing display of parallel and intersecting geometry echoed in the parallel grooves of the framework. There is a tension created by the fragile quality of glass and the cantilevered structure.

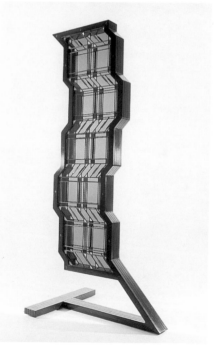
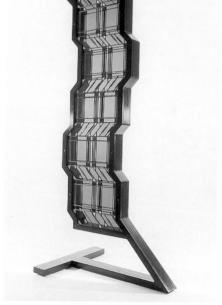

PROJECT: "Three Figures"

CLIENT: Imperial Bank

SIZE: 18 feet x 8 feet x 5 inches (5.4 meters x 2.4 meters x 12.7 centimeters)

LOCATION: Oakland, California

This lobby wall piece uses leaded glass and zolotoned wood. The three 18-feet-tall (5.4-meter-tall) bas-relief figures are rendered in iridescent, mirrored, and opaque glass chosen for its reflective light characteristics. Viewers descending the staircase see quietly shimmering highlights as their vantage point changes.

PROJECT: *Italian Cemetery Mausoleum Chapel*

CLIENT: *Italian Cemetery*

SIZE: *1200 square feet (108 square meters)*

LOCATION: *Colma, California*

ARCHITECT: *Robert Overstreet*

The building consists of a central chapel flanked by two side bays. The three-dimensional configuration of the entrance offers a changing perspective as one moves inside the building, allowing a view through one window into another. A large cross of cast glass floats overhead at the rear of the chamber in front of massive blocks of beveled and engraved plate glass. The smaller side bays echo the theme with brighter clearer tones. Cast shadows and reflections in the highly polished marble add an intricate geometric overlay that shifts with the changing light and seasons. The overall mood is one of solemn, stately peace.

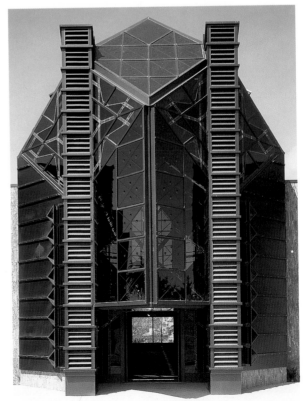

PROJECT: *"Great Reef Barrier"*

CLIENT: *Serfin Bank*

SIZE: *39 feet x 10 1/4 feet x 2 inches*
(12 meters x 3.2 meters x 5 centimeters)

LOCATION: *Mexico City, Mexico*

ARCHITECTS: *Juan Sordo Madaleno, Jorge Loyzaga*

The "Great Reef Barrier" is a three-section mural
installed on two opposite walls and the ceiling.
Suspended in a curved manner, the thirty glass pieces
recreate the colors, textures, and shapes of the sea
bottom.

Bosque de Tamarindos 17-1102

Col. Bosques de la Lomas

Cuajimalpa 05120 Mexico, D.F., Mexico

52 5 394 1319 • 52 5 570 7262 phone •

52 5 570 7202 fax

Raquel *Stolarski-Assael*

An independent artist trained in Mexico and the United States, Raquel has worked with plate glass for seventeen years. In her studio, she designs and fabricates a diverse artistic production based on cold working techniques, especially sandblasting. She constructs three-dimensional objects by laminating any number of plates to build up volume. Inlaid colored glass, metals, and other materials, together with deeply carved voids between the sheets, create in her work an internal geography that changes with light.

Her background as a psychologist introduces to her designs a conceptual framework where symbols, myths, rituals, and ancient cultural archetypes play a major role. In tandem with the aesthetic elements of her work, Stolarski-Assael seeks to convey a message by addressing a range of ideas, emotions, and longings; be it through figurative imagery or abstract design.

Her work includes large-scale elements incorporated with the architecture, sculptural as well as functional objects. For her, glass is a fascinating medium whose applications as architectural artworks have barely been tapped. She is continually experimenting with both creative processes and techniques. At present Stolarski-Assael is exploring the combination of flat glass with obsidian, a natural volcanic glass extensively used by pre-Columbian cultures in Mexico. Her work has been exhibited in Mexico, Europe, Japan, and the United States.

Life size painting of the mural, on paper.

(left)

PROJECT: *Penthouse banisters*

CLIENT: *Private residence*

SIZE: *4 feet x 102 feet x 2 inches (1.2 meters x 31 meters x 5 centimeters)*

LOCATION: *Mexico City, Mexico*

ARCHITECT: *Ruben Mesa*

Following the curved architecture of the room, the nineteen-piece staircase banister evolves from a spiral form, developed in the deeply caved design on each piece.

PROJECT: *Penthouse banisters; upper level*

CLIENT: *Private residence*

SIZE: *2½ feet x 31 feet x 2 inches (.8 meter x 9.5 meters x 5 centimeters)*

LOCATION: *Mexico City, Mexico*

ARCHITECT: *Ruben Mesa*

Panoramic view from living room of the staircase banister and the sixteen-piece glass banister encircling the top floor.

PROJECT: *"The Tree of Life," fountain*

CLIENT: *Silber Arquitectos*

SIZE: *7½ feet x 8 feet x 4 feet (2.2 meters x 2.3 meters x 1.2 meters)*

LOCATION: *Mexico City, Mexico*

ARCHITECTS: *Sergio Silberstein, Ruben Mesa*

The "Tree of Life," a candelabra cactus made up of eight glass plates, is placed on a fountain at the lobby's center, and represents Creation: the universe, humanity and knowledge; and is inspired by religions, myths, genetics, psychology, and poetry.

(right)

PROJECT: *"The Universe: The Moon"*
(detail)

CLIENT: *Silber Arquitectos*

SIZE: *4 feet x 25 feet x 2 feet*
(1.2 meters x 7.6 meters x
.6 meter)

LOCATION: *Mexico City, Mexico*

ARCHITECT: *Sergio Silberstein,*
Ruben Mesa

(above)

PROJECT: *"Samurai"*

CLIENT: *Philip and Nancy Kotler*

SIZE: *3 feet x 2 feet x 1 foot (1 meter x*
.6 meter x .3 meter)

LOCATION: *Chicago, Illinois*

The *"Samurai" resulted from a creative*
process by which drawing is done in deep
relaxation, with eyes closed and to the
rhythm of ancient music.

(bottom right)

PROJECT: *Room divider*

CLIENT: *Private residence*

SIZE: *7 ½ feet x 6 feet x 3 ¼ foot*
(2.4 meters x 1.8 meters x
1 meter)

LOCATION: *Mexico City, Mexico*

ARCHITECT: *Kaliroe Interior Design*

Includes two opposite modules between liv-
ing and dining room areas. In each, twenty-
five glass strips comprise a solid horseshoe
shape, prolonged in its two ends by a per-
pendicular plate, deeply carved on both
sides.

AFFILIATIONS

Mexican Glass Art Society
The Glass Art Society (board member 1993–1998)

PROJECT: *Synagogue Mannheim*

CLIENT: *Jewish Community*

SIZE: *Twelve windows at 9 feet x 29 feet (2.7 meters x 8.8 meters); Eight windows at 3 feet x 29 feet (1 meter x 8.8 meters)*

LOCATION: *Mannheim, Germany*

ARCHITECT: *Karl Schmucker*

The design features Desag-flashed opal glass and sandblasted floatglass, as well as opaque antique glass, flashed and etched.

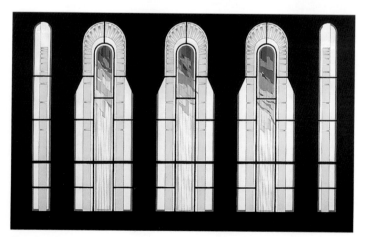

Detail of the street-side windows.

(opposite page)

PROJECT: *Theologische Hochschule*

CLIENT: *Bischöfliches Ordinariat, Limburg*

SIZE: *Twenty-four windows at 6 feet x 12½ feet (1.8 meters x 3.9 meters)*

LOCATION: *Vallendar, Germany*

ARCHITECT: *F. W. Simon, Wiesbaden, Germany*

Several of the twenty-four windows in the auditorium of the College of Theology.

Platter Strasse 96

65232 Taunusstein, Germany

49 6128 6659 phone • 49 6128 6739 fax

Karl-Heinz *Traut*

Karl-Heinz Traut attended the State Technical School for Glass in Hadamar, Germany from 1966 to 1969. After his formal training, he became the artistic manager of a big glass studio until 1977. He has since gone on to work as an independent artist and has done numerous projects for churches, and both public and private buildings.

Traut's intention is to create an intensity beyond the design surface itself to the space around his composition. His sensitivity in the use of projected light and his feeling for proportion is just as important to the successful execution of his work as his knowledge of materials and the most contemporary techniques.

Traut's concept involves paying particular attention to the differences resulting from the use of varied sizes, colors, non-colors, and density of glass. In his work, the glass very often has to be transformed by enamel paints to create harmonious color-tones. In his most recent works, the colored areas have taken on extra significance, and as a result Traut has reduced the leadline as a drawing element. Often, the leadline is even missing as an edging, so that the panes can only be adjusted and stuck together.

More than the consequence of form, Traut's work for sacral art projects is programmatic. Rather than being objectively illustrative, the subjects of his work are created in his language of form.

PROJECT: *Church St. Bonifatius, Seulberg*

CLIENT: *Catholic Community St. Bonifatius*

SIZE: *14 feet x 12 feet*
(4.1 meters x 3.6 meters)

LOCATION: *Friedrichsdorf, Germany*

ARCHITECT: *Rolf Hoechstetter, Darmstadt, Germany*

View of the chancel area.

PROJECT: *Central Office of D.A.K.*

CLIENT: *Deutsche Angestellten Krankenkasse, Hamburg*

SIZE: *63 feet x 63 feet (19 meters x 19 meters)*

LOCATION: *Hamburg, Germany*

ARCHITECT: *Pysall, Stahrenberg, and Partners, Braunschweig, Germany*

Detail of the artificially lit glass ceiling, executed from opaque glass.

PROJECT: *Matthäus Church, Wiesbaden*

CLIENT: *Protestant Matthäus Church Community, Wiesbaden*

SIZE: *17 feet x 26 feet (5.2 meters x 7.8 meters)*

LOCATION: *Wiesbaden, Germany*

ARCHITECT: *Rolf Hoechstetter, Darmstadt*

The altar window is opaque glass. The squares, letters that have been flash-removed by sandblasting, form the text of the Sermon on the Mount.

ARCHITECTURAL COMMISSIONS

Commerzbank
Hannover, Germany

Deutsche Angestellten
Krankenkasse
Hamburg, Germany

Diakonie-Anstalten
Bad Kreuznach, Germany

Dresdner Bank
Hamburg, Germany

Matthäuskirche
Wiesbaden, Germany

St. Bonifatius
Friedrichsdorf, Germany

Stadtbahn Bielefeld, Nordpark
Bielefeld, Germany

Synagogue
Mannheim, Germany

Theologische Hochschule
Vallendar, Germany

Topashaus
Leipzig, Germany

PROJECT: *Mountain View City Hall*

CLIENT: *Mountain View City Hall*

SIZE: *Interior atrium glass, four floors, 150 feet long (45 meters long) and skylight, 24 feet x 50 feet (7.2 meters x 15 meters)*

LOCATION: *Mountain View, California*

ARCHITECT: *William Turnbull Architects*

Leaded, antique, beveled, painted glass in atrium glass walls.

(opposite page)

PROJECT: *Conference room doors*

CLIENT: *Cedco*

SIZE: *6 feet x 7 feet (1.8 meters x 2.1 meters)*

LOCATION: *Louisville, Kentucky*

ARCHITECT: *Swope Design*

Conference room entry doors made of cast glass with laminated fused glass tiles and stainless steel push bars.

Architectural Glass Art, Inc.

1110 Baxter Avenue

Louisville, Kentucky 40204

502 585 5421 phone • 502 585 2808 fax

Kenneth *vonRoenn*

In addition to being a glass designer, Kenneth vonRoenn, Jr. received a Master's degree in architecture from Yale University. In his more than twenty-five years of experience he has designed more than five hundred international commissions, has been published in every major architecture magazine, including a feature article in *Architecture* magazine in January, 1992, has been the subject of several television documentaries, and has been published in numerous books.

Because of his training and practice as an architect, vonRoenn is especially concerned with the relationship between his work and the buildings of which they are a part. His ultimate objective with each commission is the harmonious integration of his

work. For this reason he approaches each project individually and develops designs that are responsive to the particular character and specific needs of each location. As a result, the evolution of his work has focused on a breadth of diverse approaches, solutions, and techniques rather than the creation of a singularly identifiable personal style.

That's not to say vonRoenn's glass work doesn't have certain visual consistencies. On the contrary, his use of glass emphasizes the structural character of the glass rather than its coloration, and he often uses glass types (such as prismatic glass) that alter and elevate the character of light. vonRoenn also is fond of using the faceted quality of prismatic glass to shape the images and views beyond the glass, creating an impressionistic, kaleidoscopic, visual distortion.

His compositions are typically expressions of dualities: structured and spontaneous, ordered and chaotic, ornamental and expressionistic. The objective of this approach is to create a rich visual dynamic as well as express the potent and vibrant quality of life; themes understood throughout time and among all cultures.

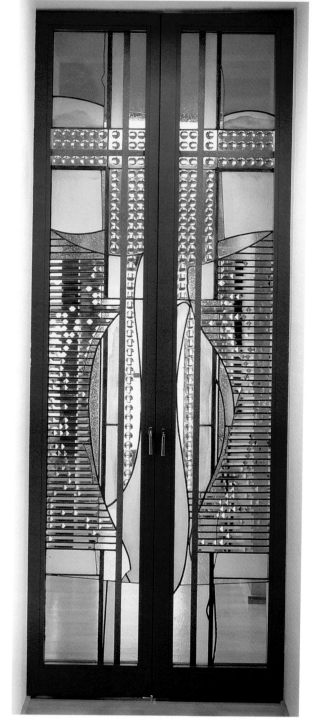

PROJECT: *Hillsborough County Government Center*

CLIENT: *Hillsborough County Government Center*

SIZE: *5 feet x 5 feet x 30 feet (1.5 meters x 1.5 meters x 9.1 meters)*

LOCATION: *Tampa, Florida*

Located 25 feet (7.5 meters) above the main entry of this government building, this curved stainless steel truss features dichroic glass forms secured above and below it.

PROJECT: *Door panels*

CLIENT: *Lustgarten residence*

SIZE: *3 ½ feet x 9 feet (1.1 meters x 2.7 meters)*

LOCATION: *Loveladies, New Jersey*

ARCHITECT: *Madden and Ryan Architects*

Leaded, beveled, and antique glass with laminated glass lenses and sandblasted, painted glass. These interior doors borrow light from the skylights beyond. The bevels and glass lenses emphasize this light as well as the background imagery.

(right)

PROJECT: *Lobby*

CLIENT: *Indiana Power and Light Company*

SIZE: *Twenty-two glass columns, each 1 foot x 2 feet x 10 feet (.3 meter x .6 meter x 3 meters)*

LOCATION: *Indianapolis, Indiana*

Glass columns composed of ½-inch (1-cm) tempered plate glass onto which are laminated beveled glass on all four surfaces and dichroic glass arcs. These glass columns are located at main entry lobby on the first and second levels, which is the primary corner of downtown Indianapolis at Monument Circle. It is quite visually prominent from the exterior.

PROJECT: *University of Toledo, School of Engineering*

CLIENT: *Ohio Arts Commission*

SIZE: *Eleven columns approximately 2 feet (.6 meter) in diameter and 10 feet (3 meters) tall*

LOCATION: *Toledo, Ohio*

ARCHITECT: *Richard Fleishman*

This piece is composed of curved laminated glass enclosing eight planes of laminated, prismatic, and dichroic glass.

ARCHITECTURAL COMMISSIONS

Al Daleel Investment & Trading Company
Riyadh, Saudi Arabia

International Monetary Fund, World Headquarters
Washington, D.C.

MD Anderson Cancer Center
Houston, Texas

Mountain View City Hall
Mountain View, California

National Airport
Washington, D.C.

Residencial Del Bosque
Mexico City, Mexico

University of Oregon
Eugene, Oregon

University of Toledo, School of Engineering
Toledo, Ohio

Wedding Chapel
Sendai City, Japan

World Ace Golf Club
Tokyo, Japan

AFFILIATIONS

American Institute of Architects

IIDA

PROJECT:	Cafeteria and lobby
CLIENT:	Merck & Co., Inc., World Headquarters
SIZE:	7 feet x 120 feet (2.1 meters x 36.6 meters)
LOCATION:	Whitehouse Station, New Jersey
ARCHITECT:	Kevin Roche, John Dinkeloo and Associates, Hamden, Connecticut

Detail from one of two enclosed dining areas in the cafeteria. Beveled and "spotted" glass is used to create a balance with the rigid geometry of the oak frame.

An interior screen between the lobby interior and the parking area (right and opposite page), shown here at night, has to work under varied light conditions.

David Wilson Design

202 Darby Road

South New Berlin, New York 13843

607 334 3015 phone • 607 334 7065 fax

David *Wilson*

Known for his large scale commissions for public and private spaces, David Wilson develops his designs with professionalism and simplicity—revealing his background in both design and fabrication. He learned to integrate these skills as a designer and later as the head of stained-glass production for a major studio in New York City. After eleven years with this company, he established himself in upstate New York as an independent designer, fabricator and installer of his leaded glass and architectural artwork. He associates with a small group of skilled artisans to execute larger projects.

Wilson's design process relies on communication and the interchange of ideas—not only with the architect designing the building, but also with those who will use the building. This reciprocal process is a delicate balance that requires mutual respect for the integrity of everyone involved.

His recent work is less concerned with isolated images than with enhancing a particular space by exploring the interface of glass art and changing light. Transformation of a flat, two-dimensional surface into something visually multidimensional is an intriguing quality of this work. Wilson manipulates transparent, beveled, and dichroic glass with opaque and/or colored glass to create depth in counterpoint to the other interior surfaces. The fragmented elements of the exterior view within his strong geometric structure create an optical weaving of light.

PROJECT: *Stamford Courthouse*

CLIENT: *State of Connecticut*

SIZE: *24 feet x 15 feet (7.3 meters x 4.6 meters)*

LOCATION: *Stamford, Connecticut*

ARCHITECT: *Ehrenkrantz & Eckstut Architects, New York, New York*

This design proposes to work within the structure of a Pilkington glass wall glazing system and retain a floating feeling of openness and light.

Full-size test panel.

Entry exterior.

PROJECT: *Entry interior*

CLIENT: *Private residence*

SIZE: *8 feet x 20 feet (2.4 meters x 6.1 meters)*

LOCATION: *Washington, D.C.*

ARCHITECT: *Cass & Associates, Washington, D.C.*

In the main entry of a private residence, etched glass is used to create privacy yet also admit optimum light.

ARCHITECTURAL COMMISSIONS

Albert Clark Residence
Cherry Hill, New Jersey
Architect: Frank Lloyd Wright

Corning, Inc.
Corporate Boardroom
New York, New York
Architect: Kevin Roche John
Dinkeloo and Associates, Hamden,
Connecticut

Immaculate Conception Cathedral
Burlington, Vermont
Architect: Edward Larrabee Barnes,
New York, New York

Ives Public Library
Percent for Art Project
New Haven, Connecticut
Architect: Hardy, Holtman, Pfeiffer
Associates,
New York, New York

La Guardia College
Percent for Art Proposal
Long Island City, New York
Architect: Warner, Burns, Toan Lunde,
New York, New York

Merck & Co. Inc.
World Headquarters
Whitehouse Station,
New Jersey
Architect: Kevin Roche John
Dinkeloo and Associates,
Hamden, Connecticut

Le Moyne College Chapel,
Syracuse, New York
Architect: Quinlivan Pierik & Krause,
Syracuse, New York

AFFILIATIONS

Graduate, Ashville College, Yorkshire, England, U.K.

Graduate, Middlesborough College of Art, Yorkshire, England, U.K. (fine arts)

Postgraduate, Central School of Arts and Crafts in London, England, U.K.
(stained glass, mural painting, and sculpture)

Gallery of Artists

Charles Z. Lawrence

PROJECT: *Abstract windows*

CLIENT: *Church of the Sacred Heart*

SIZE: *24 feet x 13½ feet (7.3 meters x 4.2 meters)*

LOCATION: *Southbury, Connecticut*

ARCHITECT: *King and Tuthill*

PROJECT: *"Ocean and Resurrection" abstract window*

CLIENT: *St. John's Episcopal Church*

SIZE: *12 feet x 6 feet (3.7 meters x 1.8 meters)*

LOCATION: *South Hampton, New York*

PROJECT: *Abstract windows over auditorium doors*

CLIENT: *Watkins Mill High School*

SIZE: *19 feet x 5 feet (5.8 meters x 1.5 meters)*

LOCATION: *Gaithersburg, Maryland*

ARCHITECT: *Duane, Elliott, Cahill, Mullineaux & Mullineaux*

Ellen Abbott and Marc Leva

PROJECT: *Moveable wall*

CLIENT: *Sultzer-Medica*

SIZE: *Six panels, 9 feet x 18 feet (2.7 meters x 5.5 meters)*

LOCATION: *Angleton, Texas*

INTERIOR DESIGN: *Nancy Taylor*

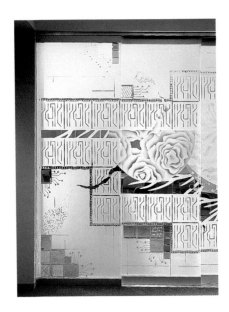

Details showing laminating.

Ellen Miret-Jayson

PROJECT: *Our Lady of the Magnificat*

SIZE: *16 feet x 40 feet (4.9 meters x 12.2 meters)*

LOCATION: *Kennelon, Kentucky*

ARCHITECT: *Michael Callori*

CLIENT: *St. Mary's Church*

LOCATION: *Portland, Connecticut*

ARCHITECT: *Pierz Associates*

CLIENT: *St. Mary's Church*

SIZE: *6 feet x 16 feet (1.8 meters x 4.9 meters)*

LOCATION: *Washington Township, Pennsylvania*

Patricia Patenaude and Frank Close

PROJECT: *Chapel Mausoleum*

CLIENT: *Lexington Cemetery*

SIZE: *6 feet x 6 feet (1.8 meters x 1.8 meters)*

LOCATION: *Lexington, Kentucky*

PROJECT: *Sanctuary windows*

CLIENT: *United Presbyterian Church*

SIZE: *10 feet x 4 feet (3 meters x 1.2 meters)*

LOCATION: *Lebanon, Kentucky*

PROJECT: *"Rise Up Singin"*

CLIENT: *OM*

SIZE: *5 feet x 4 feet (1.5 meters x 1.2 meters)*

LOCATION: *Lexington, Kentucky*

Jean Jacques Duval

PROJECT: *Leaded glass*

CLIENT: *CTK Lutheran Church*

SIZE: *2,000 square feet (180 square meters)*

LOCATION: *North Olmsted, Ohio*

ARCHITECT: *Richard Fleishman*

PROJECT: *Leaded glass*

CLIENT: *Mishran Israel*

SIZE: *10 feet x 20 feet (3 meters x 6.1 meters)*

LOCATION: *Hamden, Connecticut*

ARCHITECT: *Nathan, Bassuk Associates*

PROJECT: *Leaded glass*

CLIENT: *CVPH Hospital Interfaith Chapel*

SIZE: *20 feet x 20 feet (6.1 meters x 6.1 meters)*

LOCATION: *Plattsburgh, New York*

ARCHITECT: *Morris, Switzer & Associates*

John K. Clark

PROJECT: *Lockerbie Memorial Window, Lesser Town Hall*

CLIENT: *Scottish Metropolitan*

SIZE: *Three at 76 feet x 27 feet (23.2 meters x 8.2 meters) and three at 31 feet x 27 feet (9.4 meters x 8.2 meters)*

LOCATION: *Lockerbie, Scotland*

PROJECT: *The Dome Above the Arc*

CLIENT: *Queens Park Synagogue*

SIZE: *67 square feet (6 square meters)*

LOCATION: *Glasgow, Scotland*

ARCHITECT: *Ninian McWhannell*

PROJECT: *Old Testament Themes*

CLIENT: *St. Konrad Kirche*

SIZE: *100 square feet (9 square meters)*

LOCATION: *Amberg, Bavaria, Germany*

Paul Housberg

PROJECT: *Pfizer Central Research*

CLIENT: *Pfizer Inc.*

SIZE: *12 feet x 11 feet x 4 inches (3.6 meters x 3.3 meters x .1 meter)*

LOCATION: *Groton, Connecticut*

ARCHITECT: *CUH2A, Princeton, New Jersey*

Robert R. Pinart

PROJECT: *"A Hymn to the Joy"*

CLIENT: *Saint Francis of Assissi*

SIZE: *12 feet x 5 feet, 7 feet at top (3.7 meters x 1.5 meters, 2.1 meters at top)*

LOCATION: *Windsor, Vermont*

PROJECT: *"Repentance"*

CLIENT: *New City Jewish Center*

SIZE: *12 feet x 4½ feet (3.7 meters x 1.4 meters)*

LOCATION: *New York, New York*

Thierry Boissel

PROJECT: *Herzogschloß Straubing*

CLIENT: *Finanzbauamt Passau–*
Freistaat Bayern

SIZE: *12 feet x 23 feet*
(3.6 meters x 7 meters)

LOCATION: *Straubing, Germany*

ARCHITECT: *Finanzbauamt Passau–*
H. Kinateder and H. Mörtl

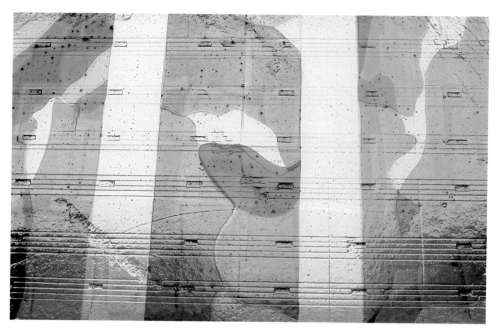

PROJECT: *Herz Jesu Kirche*

CLIENT: *Kath. Kapellengemeinde*
Zum hl. Herzen Jesu

SIZE: *Three windows,*
each 18 ½ feet x 4 feet
(5.6 meters x 1.2 meters)
one door, 10 ½ feet x 3 feet
(3.2 meters x 1 meter)

LOCATION: *Fulda-Bernhards, Germany*

ARCHITECT: *Heinz Wolf*

Detail.

Kathy Barnard

PROJECT: *"Waters of Blue Stream"*

CLIENT: *Hyatt Regency*

SIZE: *11 feet x 8 feet (3.4 meters x 2.4 meters)*

LOCATION: *Kansas City, Missouri*

ARCHITECT: *Barb Engler Crown Center Redevelopment Corporation*

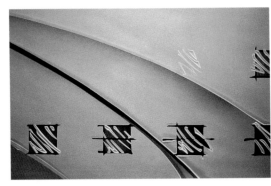

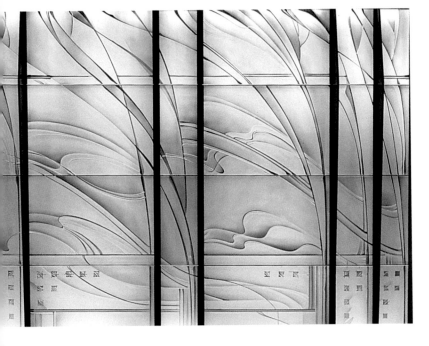

PROJECT: *"Prairie Storm"*

CLIENT: *Hyatt Regency Hotel Crown Center Complex*

SIZE: *11 feet x 8 feet (3.4 meters x 2.4 meters)*

LOCATION: *Kansas City, Missouri*

ARCHITECT: *Barb Engler Crown Center Redevelopment Corporation*

Yoshiko Takikawa

PROJECT: *"Subterranean Rainbow"*

CLIENT: *Asahi Glass Co., Ltd. and City of Nagoya*

SIZE: *5¼ feet x 62¼ feet (1.6 meters x 19 meters)*

LOCATION: *Nakamura-ku, Nagoya, Japan*

ARCHITECT: *City of Nagoya Transportation Bureau Technical Headquarters, Rapid Transit Railway Construction Architecture Division*

PROJECT: *"Film Glass"*

CLIENT: *The artist*

SIZE: *9¼ feet x 1 foot (2.8 meters x .3 meter)*

LOCATION: *Ohta-ku, Japan*

ARCHITECT: *Yasuko Mizuno Associates*

Stuart Reid

PROJECT: *"Electra's Lament"*

CLIENT: *Private residence*

SIZE: *5 feet x 6 feet (1.5 meters x 1.8 meters)*

LOCATION: *Toronto, Ontario, Canada*

Doreen Balabanoff

PROJECT: *Donor recognition windows*

CLIENT: *Freeport/Grand River Health Centre*

SIZE: *7²⁄₃ feet x 8 feet (2.3 meters x 2.4 meters)*

LOCATION: *Kitchener, Ontario, Canada*

Directory

Ellen Abbott and Marc Leva
Custom Etched Glass
1330 Lawrence Street
Houston, Texas 77008-3830
713 864 4773 phone/fax

Kathy Barnard
2000 Grand Boulevard
Kansas City, Missouri 64108
816 472 4977 phone

Berin Behn and Jan Aspinall
Architectural Stained Glass Studio
312A Unley Road, Hyde Park 5061
Adelaide, South Australia, Australia
61 8 8272 3392 phone/fax

Alexander Beleschenko
43 Jersey Street, Hafod
Swansea, West Glamorgan
SA1 2HF Wales, United Kingdom
44 179 246 2801 phone
44 179 248 0281 fax

Joel Berman
Joel Berman Glass Studios Ltd.
#1-1244 Cartwright Street
Vancouver, British Columbia, Canada
V6H 3R8
604 684 8332 phone
888 505 GLASS toll-free
604 684 8373 fax

Thierry Boissel
Akademiestr. 2
80799 Munchen, Germany
49 89 38 52147 phone
49 89 39 5684 fax

Leifur Breidfjord
Stained Glass Artist
Laufasvegur 52
101 Reykjavik, Iceland
354 552 2352 phone
354 552 2354 fax

Wilhelm Buschulte
Obermassener Kirchweg 16A
59423 Unna, Germany
49 2303 12842 phone/fax

Ed Carpenter
1812 NW 24th Avenue
Portland, Oregon 97210
503 224 6729 phone
503 241 3142 fax

James Carpenter
James Carpenter Design Associates, Inc.
145 Hudson Street
New York, New York 10013
212 431 4318 phone
212 431 4425 fax

Warren Carther
Carther Studio, Inc.
464 Hargrave Street
Winnipeg, Manitoba, Canada
R3A 0X5
204 956 1615 phone
204 942 1434 fax

José Fernández Castrillo
Mallorca 330
08037 Barcelona, Spain
34 3 207 3302 phone
34 3 459 2057 fax

John K. Clark
Oestricherstr 20
65197 Wiesbaden, Germany
49 611 941 0452 phone/fax

Brian Clarke
Toni Shafrazi Gallery
119 Wooster Street
New York, New York 10012
212 274 9300 phone
212 334 9499 fax
TSGallery@aol.com e-mail

Martin Donlin
16 St. Catherine's
Wimborne Minster, Dorset
BH21 1BE England, United Kingdom
44 120 284 9321 phone/fax

Jean Jacques Duval
Duval Studio
River Road
Saranac, New York 12981
518 293 7827 phone/fax

Bert Glauner
Morelia Glass Design Center
Apartado Postal No. 670
58000 Morelia
Michoacàn, Mexico
52 4 323 1280 phone/fax

Karl-Martin Hartmann
Parkstrasse 97
D-65191 Wiesbaden, Germany
49 611 956 6119 phone
49 611 956 6170 fax

Lutz Haufschild
1461 Nelson Avenue
West Vancouver, British Columbia, Canada
V7T 2G9
604 926 8594 phone
604 926 9452 fax

Paul Housberg
Glass Project, Inc.
59 Tingley Street
Providence, Rhode Island 02903-1021
401 831 4880 phone

Gordon Huether
Architectural Glass Design
101 S. Coombs Street, Suite X
Napa, California 94559
707 255 5954 phone
707 255 5991 fax

Graham Jones
58 First Avenue
London SW14 8SR England
United Kingdom
44 181 876 6930 phone/fax

Shelley Jurs
Jurs Architectural Glass
4167 Wilshire Boulevard
Oakland, California 94602
510 521 7765 phone
510 531 6173 fax

Keshava (Antonio Sainz)
C/ Consejo de Ciento 111 bj.
08015 Barcelona, Spain
34 3 423 1133 phone
34 3 423 1664 fax

Joachim Klos
Buchenweg 13
41334 Nettetal-Schaag, Germany
49 2153 70836 phone/fax

Stephen Knapp
74 Commodore Road
Worcester, Massachusetts 01602
508 757 2507 phone
508 797 3228 fax

Charles Z. Lawrence
Charles Z. Lawrence Stained Glass
106 West Allen Lane
Philadelphia, Pennsylvania 19119
215 247 3985 phone
215 247 3184 fax

John Gilbert Luebtow
10954 Independence Avenue
Chatsworth, California 91311
818 718 7569 phone
818 718 2601 fax

Maureen McGuire
924 East Bethany Home Road
Phoenix, Arizona 85014
602 277 0167 phone
602 277 0203 fax

Paul Marioni and Ann Troutner
4136 Meridian Avenue North
Seattle, Washington 98103
206 633 1901 phone
206 632 1363 fax

Ellen Miret-Jayson
25 Deertail
Ramsey, New Jersey 07446
201 934 0136 phone

Jean Myers
Jean Myers Architectural Glass
11 Willotta Drive
Suisun, California 94585
707 864 3906 phone
707 864 3467 fax

Patricia Patenaude and Frank Close
Patenaude/Close Studio, Inc.
115 Grand Street
New York, New York 10013
212 925 1140 phone
212 431 3141 phone
212 431 3211 fax

David Pearl
1 Greenfield Terrace
Sketty, Swansea SA2 9BS Wales
United Kingdom
44 179 229 6458 phone/fax

Robert R. Pinart
88 High Avenue
Nyack, New York 10960
914 358 1743 phone
914 358 0850 fax

Jochem Poensgen
Heinemann-Musoge-Weg 8
59494 Soest, Germany
49 2921 73533 phone
49 2921 73731 fax

Narcissus Quagliata
25125 Santa Clara Street, #155
Hayward, California 94544
Contact: Fran Bennett
510 888 2415 phone
510 537 1412 fax

Maya Radoczy
Contemporary Art Glass
P.O. Box 31422
Seattle, Washington 98103
206 527 5022 phone
206 524 9226 fax
www.mayaglass.com website

José Antonio Rage Mafud
Calle Uno No. 4 Depto. 1
Col. San Pedro de los Pinos
03800 Mexico, D.F., Mexico
52 5 272 8674 phone/fax

Stuart Reid and Doreen Balabanoff
Architectural Stained Glass, Inc.
233 Glendonwynne Road
Toronto, Ontario, Canada M6P 3G4
416 762 7743 phone

Ludwig Schaffrath
Theodor-Seipp-Strasse 118
52477 Alsdorf-Ofden
Germany
49 2404 1243 phone
49 2404 24010 fax

Johannes Schreiter
Rothkehlchenweg 7
63225 Langen, Germany
49 6103 71468 phone/fax

Jeff G. Smith
Architectural Stained Glass, Inc.
P.O. Box 9092
Dallas, Texas 75209
214 352 5050 phone
214 827 5000 fax

Arthur Stern
Arthur Stern Studios
Architectural Glass
1075 Jackson Street
Benicia, California 94510
707 745 8480 phone/fax

Raquel Stolarski-Assael
Bosque de Tamarindos 17-1102
Col. Bosques de la Lomas
Cuajimalpa 05120 Mexico, D.F., Mexico
52 5 394 1319 phone
52 5 570 7262 phone
52 5 570 7202 fax

Yoshiko Takikawa
20-5 Minamisenzoku 2-chome
Ohta-ku, Tokyo, Japan 145
81 3 3726 3702 phone
81 3 3726 6826 fax

Karl-Heinz Traut
Platter Strasse 96
65232 Taunusstein, Germany
49 6128 6659 phone
49 6128 6739 fax

Kenneth vonRoenn
Architectural Glass Art, Inc.
1110 Baxter Avenue
Louisville, Kentucky 40204
502 585 5421 phone
502 585 2808 fax

David Wilson
David Wilson Design
202 Darby Road
South New Berlin, New York 13843
607 334 3015 phone
607 334 7065 fax

Photo Credits

Ellen Abbott and Marc Leva
Sultzer-Medica moveable wall photos
by Hester & Hardaway.

Berin Behn and Jan Aspinall
Hope Valley Lutheran Church and Community
Center photos and Adelaide Magistrates Court
Redevelopment detail photos by Berin Behn.
Hope Valley Lutheran Church and Community
Center interior overview photo by Trevor Fox.
Adelaide Magistrates Court Redevelopment
project model photo by David Campbell. ANZ
Bank Redevelopment photos by Bart Maiorana.

Joel Berman
Wall Garden Hotel photo by Dan Heringa.
Canadian Airlines International and Diversey
Corporation photos by David Whittaker. The
Young Group and BC Gas photos by Roger
Brooks.

Thierry Boissel
Herzogschloß Straubing photo by Dieter Rehm.
Herz Jesu Kirche photo by artist.

Leifur Breidfjord
"Blue Dragon" detail, "Silver from the Sea,"
"Yearning for Flight," "The Human Spirit: Past—
Present—Future," "Flags," and "Med Logum Skal
Land Byggja" photos by Leifur Porsteinsson.
"Blue Dragon" photo by artist.

Ed Carpenter
"Hanging Garden" photos by Ron Starr.
Meydenbauer Convention Center, Morgan
Library, and Oakland Federal Building photos
by artist.

James Carpenter
CTS Structural Glass Prisms photos by Balthazar
Korab. First Hawaiian Bank photos by David
Franzen. Tension net stair photos by Brian Gulick.

José Fernández Castrillo
"Ciencia Y Naturaleza," "Barcelona Olimpica," and
"Al Vent" photos by Antonio Lajusticia. "Barcelona
Olimpica" detail and "Entidad Fuera de Contexto"
photo by Josefina Moya.

Brian Clarke
Photos by Stuart Blackwood, Richard Waite, Paul
Warchol, and the Toni Shafrazi Gallery.

Lutz Haufschild
Burnaby Jamatkhana interior photos by Gary
Otte. All other photos by artist.

Paul Housberg
Pfizer Central Research photos by Chee-Heng
Yeong.

Shelley Jurs
Kaiser Permanente lobby, Kaiser medical facility,
private residence front entry, and Public Library
photos by Hugo Steccati.

Keshava (Antonio Sainz)
All photos by Juan Carlos Blanco.

Joachim Klos
St. Markus Church and St. Adelheid photos by
Sebastian Klos. St. Martin church photos by Hein
Engelskirchen. Church Christ Our Peace photo
by Wolfgang Theyssen. Police Academy photo by
Inge Bartholomé.

Stephen Knapp
All photos by artist.

Paul Marioni & Ann Troutner
"Waterwall" photos by Richard Margolis. "Shelter"
photos by Russell Johnson. "Golden Leaves" and
"Elements" photos by Roger Schreiber.

Jean Myers
Cherokee Memorial Mausoleum photos by Joel
Simon. Fuqua Industries detail, Christ the King
Catholic Community Church, and Mercy Hospital
Chapel photos by artist. Fuqua Industries photo by
Gabriel Benzur.

Patricia Patenaude and Frank Close
United Presbyterian Church photo by Walt
Roycraft. "Rise Up Singin'" photo by Scott Guyon.

David Pearl
All photos by artist.

Narcissus Quagliata
Elson residence photo by Bill Kane. Yerba Buena
parking garage photo by Christopher Yates.
"Gateway to Night" photo by Alfonso Merchand.

Maya Radoczy
Recreational Equipment Inc. photos by Mike Seidl.
"Photon Interspace" photos by Said Nuseibeh.
"Gaia Reflections" photo by James F. Wilson.
"Myth and Magic in the City" photos by Dick
Springgate.

José Antonio Rage Mafud
Cielak apartment, Cherem residence, and Fermon
apartment photos by artist. Director's Bank offices,
ING Insurance offices, and El Tizoncito photos by
Akram Saab. Martínez apartment photo by Paul
Czitrom.

Ludwig Schaffrath
St. Bernard Church, Aachen-Rott residence, St.
Leonhard Church, and St. Lioba College photos
by Inge Bartholomé. Weisbaden Town Hall and
Haus der kirchlichen Dienste photos by BBK.

Jeff G. Smith
Utah Arts Council photo by Andre Ramjoué. St.
Michael Chapel, Smith residence, and AARP
photos by artist. "The Five Books of Moses" photo
by Anice Hoachlander. "Hope Chapel" photo by
Harrison Evans.

Arthur Stern
"Sentinels," "Torchere," and "Three Figures" photos
by Blake Praytor. Kitchen window photo by artist.
"Zig Zag Frozen Music" photo by Harry Orner.
Italian Cemetery Mausoleum Chapel photos by
Larry Harrell.

Raquel Stolarski-Assael
"Great Reef Barrier," residence penthouse
banisters, "The Tree of Life," and "The Universe:
The Moon" photos by Miguel Morales. "Samurai"
photo by Bernardo Arcos. Residence room
divider photo by Norberto Juárez.

Karl-Heinz Traut
Theologische Hochschule photo by Goebel,
Gorsroth. Central Office of D.A.K. photo by BBK,
Rottweil. Matthäus Church photo by Heep.

David Wilson
Merck & Co. lobby and cafeteria and residence
entry photos by Richard Walker. Stamford
Courthouse photos by artist.

All other photographs were taken by the artist or
photo credits were not available at press time.